A Journey To The Door Of Death

By

Nancy E. Perry Ph.D.

Published by Sojourn Publishing, LLC

ISBN 978-1-62747-203-6 Paperback
ISBN 978-1-62747-332-3 Hardback
ISBN 978-1-62747-334-7 eBook

This book is dedicated to my father

Simon Warren Reichard, MD

Acknowledgements

With my deepest appreciation, I wish to thank all the people who helped me write this book. I needed a lot of emotional support, as I relived a very traumatic time in my life. Reliving the trauma I experienced was sometimes painful and draining. Yet, I felt driven to complete it.

My husband Richard was the person who stood by me throughout my revelations. He provided comfort, emotional support, encouragement to continue, as well as physical help of all kinds. Richard also read my manuscript and provided editorial advice. My children, Scott, Elaine, and Karen, freely gave encouragement, emotional support, inspiration, as well as editorial help.

Others who helped edit the book and gave helpful suggestions, encouragement, and support were: Amorette Deboer, who provided a perspective from someone in their twenties who is in the process of searching for the meaning of her own life; Dr. Eileen Sheil's insight offered the perspective of one who has found the meaning in her life as a professor at the University of Wisconsin-Milwaukee; Barbara Cerino shared her knowledge as a teacher; Lee Starr helped by using her keen discernment of errors; Ralph Huber provided advice on the style of the book; Anne Lawrence's keen ability to discover grammatical errors was invaluable; and, Christina Miccio, who was present with me during part of my journey to the door of death. Christina helped validate the accuracy of some of my memories, as I relived the many traumatic experiences from my illness and medical care.

I deeply acknowledge all the people who helped me survive my journey. They include the skilled physicians, the gentle caregivers, the church members, the friends, the alternative medical providers, the countless others whose names I never knew. The list goes on and on. I am so grateful for their help. I wish I could name them all, but that is impossible. Without them, I would have been unable to write this book.

Foreword

"If there is meaning in life at all, then there must be meaning in suffering" – Victor Frankl

The early 20th century brought new technologies to the hospital. The electrocardiograph, the x-ray, and the humble stethoscope revolutionized medicine forever. The introduction of these new technologies sparked a fiery debate between those that embraced technology and those that championed the doctor-patient relationship as the cornerstone of health care. Those advocating a scientific approach to health care believed that more data could bring physicians closer to a diagnosis and thus closer to a cure. Those advocating for a clinical approach believed that little could be gained without a meaningful relationship between the doctor and the patient.

This debate continues into the present day and has only intensified. Novel diagnostic instruments such as computed tomography (CT), magnetic resonance imaging (MRI); novel medical therapeutics such as highly active antiretroviral therapy (HAART), medications for hepatitis C, disease-modifying antirheumatic drugs (DMARDs); and new modalities of health care delivery such as the electronic medical record system have improved our ability to detect and treat disease to an unprecedented degree. And yet, some argue that our diagnostic tests and our automated systems have widened the divide between doctor and patient.

In understanding this debate, scientific studies and academic papers can only take us so far. At some point we must lend our ears to those patients that have navigated our complex system. In her book, *A Journey to the Door of Death,* Dr. Perry does just this. She bravely encourages us to join her as she receives a rare medical diagnosis and is forced to change from a health care provider to a health care recipient.

By documenting the emotional journey of her treatment, Dr. Perry allows us a unique glimpse into the experience of the health-care-practitioner-turned-patient. While no age-old debates are put to rest,

Dr. Perry helps us understand that excellent health care is a crucial mix of wisdom and compassion. The world renowned surgeon, the advanced diagnostic tests, the gentle nurse who showered her after her surgery, and the family and church members that came to her aid, all play essential roles in her treatment.

Dr. Perry takes this a step further. Like many patients with complex medical issues, Dr. Perry's issues brought her face-to-face with her own mortality and her own concept of herself. In an exercise of radical honesty, she shares how her medical issues shattered several misconceptions or "myths" about herself, that then allowed for greater self evolution. She uses these experiences to formulate a theory of mythical evolution that may be used by future patients and others in order to cope with the personal changes that come with illness and suffering.

This book can lend perspective to both those navigating the health care system and to those who work in health care every day. As a physician, this book gave me greater insight into the patient experience and I am sure that it can do the same for you.

Vincent F. Miccio, Jr. MD
Pain Medicine Fellow
Columbia University Medical Center

Table of Contents

Introduction

This book is not only an account of facts and events, but is one of personal experiences. It relates to events that millions of people have lived through and continue to experience during and after an unexpected health crisis. Similar experiences to mine happen to many others as they receive life-saving medical procedures in hospitals, clinics, at the scene of an accident, in their own home, or elsewhere.

This is the inside story of a physical catastrophe that resulted in a life-changing handicap. It is also an inside story about suffering and its inevitability in everyone's life. This book's major focus is on the suffering experienced from the traumas of catastrophic illness and life-saving treatment. As a result of the physical and emotional pain I experienced, I struggled to find meanings related to my suffering that might help others in some way. So, I decided to explore answers to the following questions: How may traumatic medical events be experienced or reflected in the minds and bodies of the people who experience them? Can these experiences actually cause Post Traumatic Stress Disorder (PTSD)? What effects can result spiritually and emotionally as a result of this type of trauma? Why do some people emerge from these traumatic experiences and return to functional living while others do not? Can traumatic unexpected medical events create an existential crisis for the patient experiencing them? What are the long term effects of such a crisis? What are some of the possible psychological impacts, positive or negative, that can occur after a major health crisis? What can be done to prevent catastrophic outcomes for patients? Are there treatments available for traumatized patients? What is the impact of these events upon consciousness and personal growth?

An outsider is someone who has not actually experienced the pain these types of events can elicit within a patient. They may be unable, or find it difficult to perceive, what a victim of a sudden, unexpected medical catastrophe is experiencing. Outsiders may know little of the difficult struggles for existence that often rage within the minds of those who are experiencing a traumatic health crisis.

When communicating the experiences of my traumatic health crisis, I elected to write much of this book in the first person, present tense. I wanted to help readers better understand how patients experience both medical treatment and the professional support necessary to help them reconfigure their lives and heal.

While there are voluminous medical records of patient care related to all sorts of medical conditions, the information in this book should be understood that it is part of one individual's experience. Both health-care workers and patients can realize the impact of the relationship between the commonalities of traumatic medical treatment and related patient perceptions, as well as the coping strategies necessary for patient survival. This knowledge will aid health care workers in their efforts to help their patients.

Patients who are experiencing, or have experienced medical traumas in the past, can better deal with their sufferings and meanings of their sufferings with more self-understanding. As they become aware of new methods of self-support, they can not only survive, but thrive, while they are moving forward into the future.

Other issues related to these types of trauma are, the meanings of suffering to each individual as well as the spiritual questions that inevitably arise during and after experiencing traumatic medical and life threatening events.

A framework, in the form of a new model, emerged while this book was being written and is fully described. My model of progressive myths adds perspective to the existential questions that arise when an individual's perception of their present reality is shattered by traumatic experiences. It provides enhanced understanding of the sometimes hidden benefits of experiencing a major crisis and is based on the "myths" within which we all live.

If an individual is able to apply this model to their own life, it can enable them to better empathize with others as well as, develop a broader perspective from which to understand and reconfigure their own sufferings.

It is difficult to present a completely scientific presentation of this topic as scientific detachment is necessary for unbiased reporting. Inevitably, some of the judgements I report may not be objective and feelings I express could be out of proportion. I have attempted to avoid bias. The names of personal friends or patients have been changed to protect their privacy.

I first intended to write this book as a novel, but concluded that it would lose some of its value in that style. This story is about my experiences as I struggled through a battle to live and later deal with a resulting handicap. Before it began, I was an "outsider."

CHAPTER 1
Beginning of the Struggle

I have not been feeling well for about two weeks and am experiencing a strange anxiety, even though I know I have nothing to be anxious about. I feel somewhat "headachy," but choose to ignore it. However, something tells me it is important that I check my blood pressure, so I decide to take my blood pressure with the personal blood pressure monitor I had purchased at Walgreen's on a fateful day a week earlier.

I place the monitor on my dining room table, put the blood pressure cuff around my arm, fasten it securely, and press the button that causes the cuff to inflate and register my blood pressure. I feel fairly calm as my blood pressure has always been normal. (When I had physical exams, it usually registered slightly lower than normal at 110/60.) The new monitor registers 275/175! I feel a lightning bolt of shock go through my body. A blood pressure this high could not be possible, as I would surely have had a stroke and died before it got this high. I have never seen anyone's blood pressure this high! (I am a registered nurse and a clinical psychologist and know about these things.) The machine must be broken! I check the batteries, thump it a few times and decide to take my blood pressure again. I proceed to take it about ten more times. Each time, it registers a little higher. My calmness totally disappears as my anxiety grows with each trial. It now registers 300/175! This reading, I believe, is impossible. There has to be something wrong with the machine! Normal blood pressure is 120/80. My heart is pounding and I have developed a blinding headache. Then, I realize that I need help. I need someone to be with me and help me figure this out. I am panicked and for a few minutes cannot decide what to do, as I have no close family and only a few new friends in my new location. (I am a newcomer to Santa Fe and have only been here for about a year. I left Milwaukee, Wisconsin after a period of grieving for my husband who died unexpectedly of a heart attack four years earlier. The move was a much needed new beginning that took me away from the familiar things in Milwaukee that constantly reminded me of my grief.)

I think about calling 911, but decide instead, to call my new friend Brian, who had just shared dinner with me earlier this evening. I am struggling to calm myself enough to look up his telephone number, and am now finally calling him. I am explaining what has happened and I end our conversation by asking him to, "Please come over to my home as quickly as possible to test this machine and see if it is malfunctioning!" (I still don't think anyone can be alive with a blood pressure this high.)

As I wait for Brian to get to my house, I begin to recall events from my recent past. Maybe this will help me figure out why my blood pressure is so high. I remember that on a hike a few days ago I first noticed I was not feeling well. I had been feeling anxious for no reason and realized that my energy level was low, which was unusual for me. I had nothing to be anxious about and had no reason to feel exhausted. I also remember looking down at the glittering sand dunes in northern New Mexico where I was walking, and realizing that I was not enjoying myself. The air was cool and the sun not too bright, but I felt hot. I had been very busy for the last few days and decided to take Excedrin for some headaches that I had been experiencing for the last several weeks. I had even planned to work with several clients as well as spend time with some of my new friends when I got home from my hike, but didn't feel like doing anything. I am wondering if I subconsciously wanted to put off testing my new blood pressure monitor for some reason.

This evening at dinner with Brian, I was especially exhausted and again somewhat anxious for no reason. I am thinking perhaps the altitude is causing some of my problems. (Santa Fe is 7500 feet above sea level.) After Brian left, I prepared for bed and it was only then, that I decided to get out my blood pressure monitor to make sure my blood pressure was normal.

As I continue to review the recent past, I realize that the headaches that I have been having off and on for the last several weeks were something I had never experienced before and had chosen to ignore.

My health has always been so robust; something I automatically took for granted.

Before this experience with the blood pressure monitor, I believed myself to be almost invulnerable to any major illness and viewed myself as a person of extreme stability, peace, and calm. I experienced myself as this way for most of my life, including during emergencies. My work as a clinical psychologist has been dedicated to helping others who have experienced sudden, debilitating trauma. This is a totally new experience for me, to be in dire need of help for myself. I am continuing to review my recent past, realizing that I am trying to make sense of what is happening to me now.

My anxiety suddenly becomes almost overwhelming. I am terrified! Thoughts, like wild horses, begin to gallop through my mind, as I feel helpless for the first time in my adult memory. My mind is wandering again and again as it begins to analyze itself. I know this is probably my continuing effort to try to find a solution to my problem, to make sense of this new feeling of helplessness.

I am accustomed to believing that I can control almost everything in my life, including my physical health. I have always been a "high achiever." (In my childhood I accidentally discovered several methods that I kept secret over the years to deal with any physical problems that occurred.) My secrecy grew, as I grew, and I began to realize that most professionals, such as physicians, many nurses, and psychologists, were not only uninterested in different approaches to healing, but could also be hypercritical or even vindictive when anyone suggested approaches other than traditional procedures. I feared criticism or even censure for my lifelong interest in some of the alternatives to traditional medicine that I have explored in various ways. (I even completed training in many of them.) Since I am an experiential learner, I enjoyed learning by doing. It is so exciting to freely explore new horizons for the purpose of learning. It is very important to me to maintain a healthy scientific skepticism. I know that the scientific approach is the only way to decide if anything really works and am aware that results can be skewed by a myriad of causes. As I think of all these things, I am wondering if some of the alternative methods I learned then, can help me now.

As I continue to explore these free floating thoughts, I am interrupted by my doorbell ringing. Finally, it is Brian! Brian, who had been home and in bed when I called, dressed quickly and is now ringing my doorbell within 15 minutes of my call. (I realize that I have been attempting to control my anxiety by thinking of other things.) It has been so difficult for me to focus my mind elsewhere!

My anxiety is now forcing me back into the present. I am helping Brian take his own blood pressure. It is normal! When I retake mine again, it is even higher than before. (I don't remember how high it got.) I am shaking with terror, as I call the emergency room at our local hospital and tell them I am coming in, and how high my blood pressure is registering. I am fully aware that traditional medicine is the only thing that can help me now as I am incapable of relaxing enough to allow my blood pressure to lower itself. I know that I can die at any moment. Brian appears calm now, as he is driving me to the hospital emergency room. Thankfully, he stays with me during the drama that follows.

Reactions Experienced When Facing Death

Elizabeth Kubler-Ross is well known for her pioneering work with death and dying. She presented five stages that individuals may experience when threatened by death. They are: Denial, Anger, Bargaining, Depression, and Acceptance. Denial may occur shortly after the realization that death is probable. During this phase patients deny their reality. Anger often emerges against someone or something, to blame for their situation. Patients may become angry at God, their doctors, themselves, or anyone else. Bargaining is the phase when the patient may bargain with God and promise something such as, "If you only let me live, I will never smoke again," or "I will donate money to the poor." Depression usually occurs at some point during the process of accepting death. Acceptance during this phase indicates that the patient accepts the inevitability of their death.

Kubler-Ross did not differentiate between the victims of sudden medical catastrophes and those who have time to ponder a terminal medical illness. Victims of sudden life threatening medical catastrophes can traverse Kubler-Ross's aforementioned phases so quickly, they become almost indiscernible.

I know I have accepted the gravity of my situation. I am now impelled to deal with the existential questions that are important to complete before I die. I also must decide if I have any reason to live. I wonder if I have achieved my life's mission. The three major questions that I, and others, must answer when facing death are: What is my relationship to a higher power? Is there really life after death? and, What is the meaning of my life?

The nurse at the desk is taking me to an examining room, even before I have a chance to sit down in the waiting room. They were expecting me after my call. I am so thankful, and relieved that they know I am like a ticking time bomb that can explode and have a stroke or heart attack at any moment. Almost immediately, I see a doctor hurrying through the door! I'm so glad to see him! The nurse is taking my blood pressure again. As I look at the monitor, I see that it is registering 300/175 again. I tell myself that it is that high, partly because of my terror. (I am aware that I know too much because I am a nurse, and that makes my anxiety worse. Anxiety raises blood pressure.) My head is now pounding with almost unbearable pain. I feel like screaming, but I am going to hold it in, as I don't want to make a spectacle of myself.

The nurse is now placing a needle in my arm to keep my veins open for whatever medication they will give me. A tubing is connected to the needle at one end and the other to a liter of normal saline which is hanging on a pole. The nurse is now injecting medication into the needle. I am feeling hopeful. The medicine should bring my blood pressure right down. The doctor is staying by my side. He is saying in a reassuring voice, "Don't worry, It will come down within a few minutes." I mistakenly believe this is true.

CHAPTER 2
The Struggle Intensifies

The emergency room doctor is continuing to reassure me saying "You will probably be able to go home after about an hour." My blood pressure does go down considerably, and the pain in my head recedes somewhat. I am feeling a bit surprised as it only goes down to 220/140. I'm beginning to feel safer and am waiting for it to go down to normal. (I know the lower number has to be below 100.) The doctors and nurses are waiting too. Now they have stopped reassuring me and are adding another drug, then a third, and finally, a fourth. My blood pressure refuses to go down further. The doctor and nurse look puzzled. I overhear them saying to each other that they have not seen anything like this before. (I haven't either, of course.)

After about four hours of trying various drugs to lower my blood pressure, the doctor is telling me that I must be admitted to the hospital. He is saying, "You will be in an intensive care room, as you are still in extreme danger of having a stroke or heart attack."

Before I can fully assimilate what he is saying, I find myself being quickly helped onto a stretcher and now I am being wheeled to the intensive care room. This is all happening so quickly! I thought all would be well, if I just got to the emergency room in time. Now, my mind is having trouble absorbing all that has happened.

I am in a hospital bed in this intensive care room. My abject terror has passed and I realize that I now have time to consider more logically, for the second time in my life, the real possibility that I might not survive. This is real and true! It has all happened so fast!

I desperately want to escape emotionally from this frightening situation. I want to make sense out of what is happening in the here and now. I am again trying to make a conscious decision to escape my anxiety by thinking of other things. Part of me wonders if I am thinking these thoughts because I am getting ready to die. (I don't yet realize how rapidly I am losing my status as an outsider.) I begin to review my life and suddenly remember a major event from the past that had become a cornerstone for my life. Strangely, I now feel compelled to explore what my life has been all about.

The Christmas Present

It was Christmas! I was four years old. As I awoke, I looked out the window and was thrilled to see that snow was on the ground. I jumped out of bed and ran downstairs to see if Santa had come during the night. Our Christmas tree was lit with different colored lights. I still remember the strings of popcorn and tinsel adorning it. I knew Santa had been there as there were many presents under the tree that had not been there the night before.

I only remember two gifts. The first was a set of roller skates that I had told Santa I wanted. The second was something else that I had not asked for, but will never forget! It was a doctor's kit that, at first sight, looked like a miniature of the one my father carried. It was black and had a handle just like my father's. Since my father was a doctor, he often told me about how he had to leave to go to people's houses when they were sick to help them get well. He was sometimes called out in the middle of the night and always carried his black bag with him.

I still remember opening that unexpected package with a sense of sheer delight. I wanted to be a doctor like my father as far back as I could remember. I idolized him and wanted to save people like he did. The stethoscope did not look exactly like my father's, but I thought it might work anyway. I could hardly wait to listen to everyone's heart as well as look into everyone's throat! I needed to ask my father how the thermometer worked.

My reverie is interrupted as I am suddenly drawn back to my hospital surroundings in the here and now. A nurse is next to my bed, insisting I take a sleeping pill. Even though I never use sleeping pills, I agree, as I know if I do not take it, I will be awake all night, thinking about my mortality. As I lay my weary head down in my hospital bed, I am consciously observing my thoughts and feelings as the sleeping pill takes effect. The desire to explore one's relationship to God is a normal reaction when faced with one's own mortality. When accepting the reality of one's death, people inevitably wonder if there really is life after death and are often drawn to explore the meaning of their life.

Ascertaining my Relationship to a Higher Power

Two questions that emerge for me and almost everyone close to the door of death are: Who or what is God? Is there really a God? I am thinking of the following quotes by Albert Einstein: In 1970 he was quoted as saying "I believe in Spinoza's God who reveals himself in the orderly harmony of what exists, not in a God who concerns himself with fates and actions of human beings." In a 1929 interview with the *Saturday Evening Post* he stated, "Let us not forget that knowledge and skills alone cannot lead humanity to a happy and dignified life. Humanity has every reason to place the proclaimers of high moral standards and values above the discoverers of objective truth. What humanity owes to personalities like Buddha, Moses, and Jesus ranks for me higher than all the achievements of the inquiring and constructive mind." I have always been aware that there are many definitions of God and am stimulated to ponder my own beliefs.

I, and other human beings who are consciously aware of facing death, report some of the following thoughts about God. As I observe my thoughts, I am aware that I am wondering how God could have allowed this to happen to me. Is he or she helping me now? If so, how? I am continuing to pursue these questions when my mind wanders and finds itself changing my perception of God as I am aware of my own impending death.

Now that I am facing death, I realize that I have not been thinking much about God in the recent past, but know that I believe in a higher power. I have meditated and prayed regularly for many years. As I face death I know that I must decide what or who God really is for me.

I am a little surprised and happy to wake up in the morning! I suddenly remember that I am in an intensive care room. Brian is not here, but said he would return this morning. My blood pressure is still dangerously high, but I am alive! A woman in a pink uniform is entering my room with what looks like some kind of drink in a tall glass which she places on a doily. There is also a glass of apple juice. She is announcing, "You are on a liquid diet." I didn't know that, but think it's probably been ordered for some good reason.

Suddenly, I feel a sharp pain in the roof of my mouth. It hurts so much! It is coming and going, like some kind of cramp. It seems to be intensifying since I drank my liquid breakfast. I'm pressing the call bell so I can tell a nurse about this terrible pain. Thank goodness, the nurse is coming right in my door. She is telling me that she will tell the doctor on call about this new development.

I think it is now about a half an hour since I told the nurse about the pain. I wish someone would come right away and help me. It is getting worse! Finally, the doctor and a nurse are entering my room. I perceive that they are looking at me quizzically as I am describing my pain. I wonder if they believe me, or if they just didn't know what to think. One nurse is telling me, "This has nothing to do with your blood pressure." They are also informing me that I will now be moved to another private room staffed with fewer intensive care nurses. I am not allowed to walk to my new room. (This further validates my belief that I am in very serious trouble.) My mind is beginning to wander again, and I wonder if there is anything I can do for myself to alleviate my intense fear.

I hope that something I learned in my training as a psychologist many years earlier will help me survive whatever is to come. That something is the practice of Mindfulness. (Mindfulness is a method that connects you with your life in the here and now.) "It is purposefully and non-judgmentally observing your awareness as if your life depended on it," states, Jon Kabat-Zinn, who teaches meditation as a basic skill to achieve mindfulness. (I learned to meditate in my early thirties. At that time Transcendental Meditation was beginning to be used to help with addictive behaviors. I also explored many other methods that could be used to meditate, and finally chose Mindfulness Meditation.) Meditation had always helped me attain a level of peace and tranquility as well as a feeling of oneness with the universe.

I am aware that, for some reason since my anxiety began, I now find it impossible to meditate. It is as though my mind is too scattered and I cannot concentrate on anything for more than a few minutes. (I have enjoyed meditating for many years, along with the awareness of observing myself.) Even though I feel trapped by my inability to concentrate now, I am somewhat relieved to find that even though I can no longer meditate, I can still accomplish mindfulness without meditation. I am aware that I have been doing this automatically since yesterday. Mindfulness involves observing yourself and all your feelings in the here and now. I believe this skill is helping me right now to make sense of what is occurring in the present, as well as helping me survive. Mindfulness is pure awareness. Meditation is one of the paths to mindfulness. The process of mindfulness enables one to be aware of oneself within the bigger picture of existence and consciousness. I am well aware that I am suffering! The pain in my mouth hurts so much, but the emotional pain in my heart from not being able to concentrate and think clearly is more painful.

Suffering

I know that I am suffering deeply in a more intense way than ever before in my life. It feels like a deep inner sadness, mixed with grief, anxiety, fear, and helplessness. I am experiencing it in my chest and brain, as well as in my heart. Sometimes I feel tearful, other times fearful. I vacillate between having an impulse to scream or to cry. I wish I could run away from it all, but have nowhere to go.

My analytical mind is able to take me out of my suffering for a few minutes, when I begin to become mindful and analyze myself and my situation. I am thinking about how, when we experiences suffering as well as the possibility of death, we often automatically review our life and attempt to understand the meaning of it. I well know from my work, that everyone experiences suffering in their lives. It is inescapable. We all experience old age, emotional pain, and various losses. Family members and friends die. Everyone can lose jobs, love, homes, security, and friends, to name a few. All relationships end, whether, by rejection, divorce, or death. It is normal to have a fear of death. Suffering is part of living. Nietzsche once said, "What does not kill us makes us stronger." When I think of this, I wonder how or if I will be stronger, if I do survive.

Extreme suffering occurs in hospital settings every day. Suffering is traumatic not only for everyone who experiences it, but also for their loved ones who are observing it. Medical conditions and their treatments can result in trauma significant enough to cause Post Traumatic Stress Disorder (PTSD). (PTSD is a condition most readers are familiar with. It is often experienced by soldiers returning from war.) My mindful self observes that I am becoming traumatized by my situation. I am not sure if this awareness is helping me, or making me feel worse.

My Suffering as a Catalyst to Growth

Suffering creates a crisis in one's life. Some children experience child abuse or handicaps so devastating, that they begin their suffering soon after birth. Others experience physical and emotional trauma from different sources such as war, domestic violence, auto accidents, attack, major hospitalizations, etc. Watching or even hearing of someone else's trauma can cause secondary PTSD. It is even possible to become traumatized and suffer by watching graphic videos on the news of the suffering of others. This was recently exemplified by a video of immigrants from Syria who were on a boat that capsized. It showed a father holding his dead children and crying for them and his drowned wife. Every day many people experience traumatic events and suffering in hospitals. These events are powerful enough to cause PTSD. The crises caused by suffering offer an opportunity to grow and change. I know all this, but cannot yet identify how this can happen for me.

Various specialists are coming and going. I am exhausted from giving my medical history over and over. No one seems to care about the terrible pain in my mouth. It has become so intense that I have to cry out when it arrives. It is now happening every five minutes and lasts about a minute. I am now timing it on my watch and finally, am begging for an Eye, Ear, Nose, and Throat specialist (EENT) to come and examine my mouth. The doctor on call agrees, and the EENT specialist is scheduled to arrive later this afternoon.

A doctor I have not seen before is entering my room. He is introducing himself as the EENT specialist. I am not in pain right now. (It is the in-between time when I can be comfortable.) I am trying to calmly describe to him what is happening in my mouth even though I am scared. Now he is giving me the same quizzical look the other doctors and nurses have given me. Suddenly, the pain begins to recur in its same timely manner. I begin to grimace, tears involuntarily running down my cheeks, as I struggle to hold back the screams I can feel building within me. All I can manage to say is, "Here it comes!" The doctor yells, "Open your mouth!" It is so hard to do, but I do it. As he looks in my mouth with his light, I hear him mumbling, "Oh my

God." He continues watching for the entire one minute of my excruciating pain which finally begins to subside, leaving me weak and sweaty, but somewhat relieved that someone has now witnessed that something terrible is wrenching the life from me. (The doctor had seen actual muscle spasms occurring in my mouth) He says, "I am ordering an immediate MRI (Magnetic Resonance Imaging) of your head and neck."

CHAPTER 3
The Cataclysm

I know this means I will be placed in a machine where magnetic waves can show any irregularities in the tissues in my head and neck. By this time I only want the pain in my mouth to stop. I am again focusing on my mortality, realizing that I am not sure in this moment if I will live. If I have to die soon, I somehow know that I must quickly discover the meaning of my life. (My mind begins to wander away from my here-and-now suffering.)

I remember Victor Frankl's 1959 book, *Man's Search for Meaning,* which I read in graduate school. It was about Frankl's experiences in German concentration camps during the Second World War. He discovered that people who experienced meaning in their life tended to survive better than those without meaning. (I realize that I have involuntarily been pondering the meaning of my life and fleetingly hope that this will somehow help save me.) I am also thinking about how the concept of resiliency connects with Frankl's search for meaning. Resiliency is best described as the process experienced by people who do not let adversity define them. It is an ability to cope with, and survive, various types of suffering. People who are resilient understand and accept that physical and emotional suffering happens. They are able to reconstruct their lives and survive. I wonder if I am resilient enough to survive and recover from my present dilemma, or if survival is possible at all.

I am beginning to think about my past again, as I ponder the experiences that I and others have reported when considering their life's purpose. I find myself returning to the time in my early childhood when I received that doctor's kit.

The Commitment

I carried that doctor's kit with me everywhere I went, for at least a week. I then organized it so it would be ready if anyone got hurt and placed it in the closet in my bedroom so I could get it quickly if needed. I remember the excitement I felt as I waited for the opportunity to actually help someone! It was truly the beginning of my growing awareness that healing would be my life's work. I had not yet understood how fortunate I was to realize what my mission in life was to be, beginning at the age of four. That was just the beginning of my search for ways to heal others. I wanted to help others like my father did, but was not yet aware how that Christmas gift would affect the rest of my life. My life had been placed on the course of becoming a healer, a path from which I never deviated.

As I think of my life commitment to healing others, I am suddenly brought back from these thoughts by words from my EENT doctor. It is so difficult to stay in the present. He says, "I am prescribing a very strong pain killer called Neurontin, which I believe, will take away the pain in your mouth." The Neurontin soon arrives from the pharmacy and even though I've always avoided painkillers, I find myself eagerly swallowing the pills.

Its effects are finally beginning to deaden my pain. I'm waiting now to experience the MRI. My pain was so excruciating, I am willing to take almost anything to alleviate it.

It is now about an hour since I took the Neurontin. The periodic pain in my mouth has receded. However, I'm starting to see halos around everything and I feel somewhat dazed, although still anxious. I can now barely concentrate on anything, but am realizing that my anxiety is now appropriate for my situation. (I am not yet aware what the price of relieving my pain will cost me.)

I have never experienced an MRI before, but know that some people become claustrophobic when they are placed inside the MRI machine. (As a psychologist I have taught a number of people how to relieve claustrophobic feelings through the use of self-hypnosis.) Even though I am a bit dazed from the pain killing drug, I am still trying to reassure myself that down deep, my true personality is that of a basically calm, well-adjusted person. I believe the MRI will not bother me at all. I know I cannot concentrate well enough to accomplish self-hypnosis. I believe I can do it without hypnosis!

Two burley male attendants are entering my room to take me to my MRI scan. Surprising to me, they are rolling my entire bed, with me in it, down the hall and into an elevator, so I can be taken to another floor. This further alarms me as I know I must really be seriously ill, otherwise they would use a wheel chair.

We have arrived at the MRI room, and the attendants are gently lifting me to a platform that will later slide into the MRI machine. I am now lying flat on my back. The MRI technician is placing a rigid helmet around my head and neck. It has a mask-like apparatus that fits over my face and is so tightly screwed together, it is pressing slightly into my nose. The only movements I can accomplish are to open and close my eyes and mouth, swallow, talk, and perhaps twitch my nose against the rigid structure encasing me. I cannot move my head or neck at all and my arms have to be kept close to my sides. The technician is pressing a button and the platform slides into the machine. I have a rubber bulb in my hand that I can squeeze, if for some reason, I panic. I know that if I do this, the whole session will be ruined and I would then be heavily sedated to repeat the whole procedure. Part of me feels like screaming, but I am able to control myself by deep breathing exercises I learned long ago and often taught others.

Since I learned early in my work as a therapist how to be mindful, observing my feelings continues to help me gain more control of them. Even though I have treated many patients over the years who needed to cope with fears of MRIs and radiation treatments, by teaching them self-hypnosis, imagery, and relaxation techniques, I did not really know how these procedures felt. I could only imagine it, as I was an outsider. I realize that now, I am discovering firsthand how these procedures actually feel.

I am continually surprised that it is difficult or impossible for me to use some of the techniques I have taught to so many others. I believe that this is because I can no longer concentrate for longer than a few minutes. I have no further doubt in my mind, that I am now an "insider" and that my belief in traditional medicine as my only hope for survival is valid.

The MRI technician seems very kind. She is explaining everything very clearly and reassuring me that she will speak to me over a speaker that is inside the machine and is also connected to the earphones she has placed in my ear canals. The earphones will block out some of the noise from the machine, as it scans my head and neck.

After the platform rolls into the machine, I am on my own. I am a little surprised that I am experiencing extreme feelings of loneliness as I feel my belly and chest tighten and I begin to become panicky. Even though I cannot concentrate on anything, I decide to try to listen to, experience, and imagine the sounds I am beginning to hear as something that is helping me. The sounds are best described as "clicking," "clacking," and "knocking." I imagine them as healing whatever problem is there, even though I know they are not really doing this. At times the technician asks me over her speaker phone, to hold my breath. During this entire experience, I realize that I am fighting the panic of claustrophobia. The exam takes almost two hours. At one point it stops briefly, as now the technician is injecting a dye in my arm to better define any problem I might have in my head and neck. As the examination is progressing, my panic level is also progressing. I am not able to access the tools I know to change my consciousness.

Consciousness

Consciousness may be simply defined as the state of being awake and aware. It is, in part, awareness by the mind of itself. Hippocrates has been quoted as saying, "Consciousness is the window through which we understand." The major factor that affects the reality of what we perceive is the accuracy of our perception. If you perceive a person has a gun when they do not, your reality is inaccurate. Your expectations, fears, vision, hearing, and current emotional state all affect your perception. I wonder if I have been misperceiving something.

Theologians, scientists, and philosophers have long debated what consciousness really is. Rene Descartes defined consciousness by saying, "I think, therefore I am." This is a very simplistic view and is limited to only knowing that one is in the world. The major question is how do we become conscious of who we really are? If the brain thinks, it may know it exists, but does not yet know who it really is.

Issues raised by philosophers and theologians include factors that may fit into quantum physics theory. One of the questions they considered involves the effects of altered states upon consciousness. These states may occur with the administration of psychedelic drugs, hypnosis, meditation, and prayer.

Many scientists believe that consciousness is only related to the physical body and resides in the brain. There is research to suggest that some of the reported near death experiences are explainable by deterioration of nerve cells in the brain shortly after death. This supports their hypothesis that consciousness ends, when the body is dead.

Theologians have differing views of consciousness, based on their particular religions. All believe in life after death, but, again may view it differently, depending on their religion. Most people are aware that there are different realities for each religion. For example, Catholics believe in Hell, Heaven and purgatory. Most Christian religions believe in life after death and some believe in the Resurrection. The resurrection is to occur on resurrection day, after Christ returns. Others reject the ideas of purgatory. Buddhists

21

believe in reincarnation. Muslims believe in the last day of judgement and the hereafter, and that everyone will be resurrected for judgment into either paradise or hell.

Some behavioral scientists, physicians, mystics, and yogis have developed different theories about consciousness. Larry Dossey and others have investigated the phenomenon of non-local mind. There is significant evidence that our minds can affect others either negatively or positively from a distance.

I am remembering a profound experience that actually happened to me, on a weekend, a number of years ago. I was teaching a three day workshop at the University of Wisconsin to physicians and nurses on how to use hypnotic techniques in hospital settings.

It was the second day of my workshop. I was leading the class in a guided imagery to better help them understand themselves as well as attain an altered state of consciousness. The exercise first involved helping everyone get into a relaxed state and then asking them to imagine some things that I would describe. First, I asked them to close their eyes, take some deep breaths, and then relax various muscle groups starting with their head and progressing to the tips of their toes. After the group was relaxed, I asked them to imagine themselves resting on a beautiful beach. (I constructed a beautiful beach in my mind as I described it to them.) Then, I helped them imagine someone walking down the beach toward them who could answer any question they wished, that they believed would help them with any problem they currently had in their life. This someone could be a religious figure, someone they knew, or someone else, entirely different. They were instructed to visualize that person, sit down with them, and ask their question. Then, they would receive the answer to that question.

All was proceeding as planned, when suddenly one woman in the workshop, whom I will call Harriet, started crying and screaming hysterically! I was astonished, as I had experienced this exercise myself several times, as well as used it, in various other hypnosis workshops before this. I had never experienced a participant reaction like hers. My assistant tried to calm her, but she became even more hysterical. Everyone in the class had opened their eyes by that time and appeared to be quite concerned. I decided to have my assistant assign a reading to the group, while I helped Harriet to another room in the building, so I could determine what was wrong, and how to help her.

I hoped to comfort her and asked what had happened during her imagery. Harriet told me that she saw her son coming down the beach to her. After they sat down, he immediately explained that he had been killed in an accident in Germany. He also told her that he loved her and had come to say, "good bye." I was almost speechless as she tearfully asked me, "Could this be true?"

Harriet was so upset that I knew she should not continue my workshop in her current emotional state. She then mentioned that her son was in the army and currently stationed in Germany. I suggested to her that she go home and try to get in touch with her son to make sure he was all right. Harriet agreed and asked me to please tell the other class members what had happened, so they could understand her hysteria. Harriet then rushed out of the room to hurry home, so she could determine if her vision was true. I wondered what had really happened and what her imagery meant. I returned to the workshop and spent some time with the class, debriefing them about what had occurred. The rest of the day passed without incident.

The next morning was the last day of the workshop. I entered the presentation room early and, to my surprise, saw Harriet sitting in a front seat, looking happy. I was also happy to see her looking so well and immediately asked her about her son.

She then told me the following story: Harriet's son John was currently stationed in Weisbaden, Germany. He had been involved in a routine training mission and had been in an accident. His heart had stopped from the trauma of the accident and he had been declared dead, exactly at the time I had been doing the imagery exercise with my class. Several minutes later he was revived and attending medics reported that it seemed as though he had "returned from the dead."

After the rest of the class filed in, I asked Harriet if she wanted to share that information with the class. She did. We were all deeply touched and amazed. What happened to cause this incident? Was this an example of non-local mind? I could think of no other explanation.

During the workshop, the consciousness of the class members had been changed, due to relaxation techniques and the use of imagery. Was it possible that Harriet's son's consciousness also changed, when his heart had actually stopped beating at that same time, allowing them to communicate?

The theory of non-local mind is well supported by research. It hypothesizes that consciousness can travel through time and space and be present not only within the brain. This theory supports the reality that prayer can actually affect the recipient of a prayer, even across long distances. Larry Dossey M.D. was a pioneer who researched this theory and considered its implications for human beings in today's world. Research has demonstrated that the essence of who we are is connected to others, no matter where they are. There is clear evidence that everyone in the world and all sentient beings are connected with each other through time and space.

I remembered that Edgar Mitchell, one of the first men on the moon, and founder of the Institute of Noetic Science, described his experience of a profound change in his consciousness. While he was observing the earth from outer space, he had the awareness that all people are actually connected to one another through consciousness. It was an epiphany for him. The Noetic Science group, of which I am a member, continues to perform significant research related to consciousness.

Many yogis believe that meditation is a way to explore the mind. Buddhist monks have long been recognized for their ability to control their emotions. They hold a key to methods that can help people deal with unpleasant emotions. Buddhist monks have been studied extensively during and after meditation. Actual physiological changes were noted and measured during their meditations. Results demonstrated that their consciousness and physical states significantly and positively changed during their meditations.

Psychologists connected with the American Psychological Association are now interested in collaborating with the monks to better understand and apply some of their methods to help others. Davidson and Harrington in their 2001 book, *Visions of Compassion: Western Scientists and Tibetan Buddhists Examine Human Nature,* explores these exciting positive results.

Meditation has been effective in treating various addictive behaviors. It calms the entire nervous system. Many people report that it helps them get in touch with the love in their heart, as well as raises their consciousness. Others sometimes experience an awareness of oneness with all things.

Psychedelic drugs can also change consciousness. Permanent changes in consciousness may remain after the effects of the drugs have worn off. Hypnosis can modify a person's perception of him or herself as well as of the world.

As consciousness grows, the question becomes, how far can it expand? Many consider the ultimate level of consciousness in this plane of existence to be "awakening" or "enlightenment." Individuals who report experiencing enlightenment describe it as being a feeling of perfect peace and love for everything and everyone in the world, with an awareness of oneness and empathy with all. Eckart Tolle describes it as almost an emptying the mind of all thought processes and being fully in the here and now. The task becomes how to widen your love, deepen your understanding, and bless the world. I wonder what level of consciousness I would have if I weren't now so drugged and helpless.

I find myself, repeatedly trying to think of things in the past and also have other theoretical and philosophical thoughts related to what I am experiencing. I am trying to distract myself, perhaps by trying to make sense out of what is happening to me. I am also wondering if my physical problems could have a psychological component of some kind. However, I cannot figure out anything that it could be in my case. I do not know of any psychological problem I could have that could be work related, but wonder if there could be something else I haven't thought about.

Something has changed! At this moment, I can no longer think about other things as well as I could a few minutes ago! I cannot distract myself. I feel trapped! I'm scared! I want to call off the MRI scan and escape from this hellish place. I know where I am in the here and now, and don't want to be here. Now it feels like torture. I am aware that I am losing my ability to think about anything in order to stop being aware of where I am in the here and now, deep within the bowels of the MRI machine. I observe, and am trying to ignore my rising sense of claustrophobia. I am now beginning to experience raw panic. It is more and more difficult to maintain control! I have almost given up hope that I can hold on to my sanity. Suddenly the technician announces over the speaker connected to my earphones, "The MRI scan is completed." (Since people who experience severe claustrophobia in MRI machines are often administered sedatives, this is an indication that the MRI test in itself may be traumatizing to many people.)

The end of the scan has finally arrived. The kind technician returns, slides me out of the capsule and begins to release me from the mask over my face. I can barely contain the tension that is exploding within me! Even though it is only a few minutes, the time it takes for her to completely remove the face mask seems interminable. My release is finally completed! I suddenly feel a huge sense of relief wash over me like a wave, but note a sad look on the technician's face as she is bidding me farewell. She quietly says, "Good luck." Her kindness touches me. I somehow feel understood. Tears are coming to my eyes and rolling down my cheeks. I'm wondering how serious her findings really are, and if her sad look is related to my condition. (I soon find out that it probably is.)

As my bed and I are now being returned to my room, my mind is wandering again and I am remembering, feeling, and thinking many things that roll through my brain in kaleidoscopic fashion. I am wondering, what could be wrong with me? Will I live through it? I am obsessing again about the real possibility that I will die and wonder over and over, if I have accomplished what I am supposed to accomplish in this lifetime. I am thinking of all the people in my life whom I love, and about my reasons to live. It is so difficult to concentrate! I wonder if there is an afterlife and what will happen to my consciousness when I die. For some reason, I want to avoid thinking about God again, but still believe that I should pray for help.

I find that I am not ready to pray yet. It doesn't feel right and I'm wondering why. I think I first need to further define what I really believe about God. (As a child, I grew up in the Methodist church and believed in a traditional God. However, my mother had been Catholic and my father Protestant. As a result, I have many Catholic and Protestant relatives, whom I love. In addition, we lived in a Jewish neighborhood, so I was exposed to the Jewish faith at an early age, respected it, and also have Jewish friends whom I love.) I am asking myself the questions: "What is God? Who is God? Does God really exist? Could atheists be right? How can God, if there really is a God, know and care about me? If God is here and knows about me, how can he or she have let this happen to me? (I have been attending the Unity Church of Santa Fe for over a year now and had begun to consider myself to be somewhat of a Christian mystic.) I so enjoy the Unity services as they are non-denominational and people from all religions are welcome. The energy of love seems to permeate the sanctuary. As I am thinking of these things here in my hospital bed, I realize that I have decided that for me right now, God is love. Love is an energy, not an entity who is vengeful, judgmental, or controlling.

As I continue to ponder what I think is my heightened spiritual awareness, I feel myself being drawn back to the present. I don't want to be pulled back. I do not want to face my present dilemma and am reluctant to return into the here-and-now. I am sad that this is so. My inability to concentrate for longer than a few minutes is such an alien experience and is extremely frustrating. I continue to feel trapped into helplessness. My strange anxiety continues to puzzle me. Could I be having an emotional breakdown of some kind? Again I almost involuntarily start to think of my life in the past, the meaning of all the things that happened to me and how they changed my life. I realize that I now have very little control of my emotions and my mind. I can no longer help anyone. I feel a surge of heightened empathy for the patients I have helped, as well as for my fellow patients right here in the hospital with me. I am now an "insider" and can better understand and empathize with how my patients must have felt during some of their medical procedures. Now, I can do nothing but just be. I cannot help anyone! I cannot even read a book, so I begin to have more musings about my past. Thinking about my future is too frightening today, as that may mean death!

My primary life's work and public persona have been dedicated to traditional medicine within the medical establishment. My work as a nurse, psychologist, and professor has required that I adhere, for the most part, to the traditional scientific paradigm.

I discovered early in my life, and know, from a scientific perspective, that the mind has a profound effect on the physical body. Part of my work has been teaching hypnosis and imagery to health care professionals at the university level. I also use hypnosis and imagery quite often in my practice to successfully treat some of the physical and emotional problems experienced by my patients. As I think of these things, my mind slips into another experience in the past, when I was six years old.

Learning to Heal Myself

I was a lonely, 'only' child. As everyone knows, 'only' children usually find themselves the major focus of their parents' attention. For me, this was magnified due to some unusual factors.

My father was a doctor, who was fifty seven years old when I was born. I was an unplanned surprise! I believed my parents were both shocked and pleased at my entrance into their lives. I was a rather precocious child and grew accustomed to being the center of their attention. They were very strict and demanded complete obedience and high achievement.

I enjoyed some of this attention, but was uncomfortable when my parents went to extremes with concerns about my health. They were over-protective in many ways, but seemed obsessed with my health. My parents were so concerned about my health that they began feeling my forehead two or three times a day to see if I had a fever. I became extremely frustrated with this, and tried to avoid their concern.

I often checked my own forehead to see if it felt hot. If it did, I would spit into my hand and rub the saliva on my forehead to cool it off before going near my parents. I knew that if I did have a hot forehead, I would have a thermometer placed in my mouth and be confined to bed. My parents would become distraught! (I felt like such a burden to them then, and could not bear to see them so upset.) At that time I remember deciding that I would do everything I could to avoid getting sick. I didn't want my parents to worry. I didn't want to be a burden and I wanted them to leave me alone and stop feeling my head.

One of the things I decided to do was to, "pray to God" to take away my fever or any pain I might be having. Sometimes that seemed to work; sometimes it didn't. If that didn't help, I thought maybe I could concentrate and make whatever was wrong "go away." I taught myself to relax and send something like "energy" or "thought" to whatever part of me hurt. (I had accidentally stumbled into methods that seemed to begin to work.) I discovered that once in a while, I could even make a sore throat go away as well as a stomach ache. Sometimes I could lower a fever. I wasn't positive it really worked, so I didn't tell my parents or anyone else, because I didn't want them to worry or think I was "weird." I was only six years old.

By the time I was in the second grade, I was better able to accomplish my secret process very well. My parents seemed relieved that I was in such good health. I decided it really worked. By the time I was in the eighth grade, I had achieved six years of perfect attendance in school. I always sent thoughts or energy to wherever I had pain and believed I actually could feel the surge of energy going to that part of my body. My parents, over-concerned about my health, inadvertently opened my mind to what, in later years, was to become Alternative or Complementary Healing Practices.

I am a little surprised to find myself in my bed back in my hospital room. I wonder if distracting myself by remembering things I have not thought of for years is emotionally healthy for me. I cannot heal myself now, as I did in the past. I realize now that I may be distracting myself for two reasons. The first, and most important to me, is to consider what my life has been all about and the second is to avoid the trauma of my present situation. It saddens me to realize that I must finally accept the fact that I must totally rely on traditional medicine alone to survive.

I remember, the MRI really is over! I feel sweaty and untidy. I'll ask the nurse if she thinks it would be safe for me to take a shower. A young attractive nurse is entering my room. She is telling me that she is assigned to me for the day and says, "Yes, a shower would be perfectly fine." I am feeling almost happy, as I gather a towel and clean pajamas and hurry into the shower room. I finally open the shower door and turn on the hot water. I'm beginning to feel the water. It is so wonderful and the temperature is just right. I haven't had a shower for days. I am luxuriating in the very warm water cascading over me.

However, something is wrong! I am becoming dizzy. My head is spinning! I feel myself falling to the floor of the shower. It is happening so fast. I realize that I may have lost consciousness for a minute or two. I am beginning to slowly regain my awareness. I can see the towel on a rack just outside the shower door. Even though I still feel a bit dizzy, I am reaching for the towel and finally wrapping it around myself. It is so hard to drag my body back to my hospital bed! I hope I can make it. I have finally reached my bed! I made it here, so I can fall into it even though I am still damp from the shower! I feel so weak and confused.

Dr. Abel, my primary care doctor, is now entering my hospital room. I don't know how long it has been since I fell into bed. She is asking me, "Why are you naked and wrapped in a wet towel?" I am explaining to her what happened and notice that she seems extremely concerned and immediately begins taking my blood pressure. It has gone down suddenly and is the cause of my collapse. The very warm water from the shower caused my blood vessels to dilate and lower my blood pressure. I am now beginning to believe that no one knows what to do to help me. I feel like sobbing, but am holding it back, as I do not want to let others see how disturbed I am.

It is now afternoon. The individual specialists are beginning to arrive. First a neurosurgeon enters the room. He is asking me the same questions I have answered many times before. A few minutes after he leaves, the EENT doctor returns to see how I am feeling. Soon another internist I do not know is entering the room and again is asking me all about my case. Dr. Abel is informing me that they are all here to help solve the mystery of what is wrong with me. It seems to me that the doctors and I are all waiting for the results of the MRI scan, hoping it will shed some light on the cause of all my problems.

Now it is finally night time. I am almost ready to prepare for the night. My door opens and Dr. Abel is entering the room. She is looking at me kindly and says gently, "I suggest that you have a family member with you for a meeting tomorrow morning with your whole medical team." I have no family members who live close enough to get here in time, so I know I am on my own. By this time, I feel sure that I am out of control of my life. Whatever is causing my problems, must be something extremely serious! I wonder again if I will live through it. I feel so alone, but grit my teeth, determined to deal alone with whatever happens.

It is morning and right after breakfast. The medical team is beginning to arrive. They come in one by one, each pulling a straight chair into my room and placing it somewhere around my bed. Now they are all assembled, sitting quietly, all looking at me with solemn expressions on their faces. I am aware that they seem somewhat nervous. All four doctors are here. The EENT specialist is speaking first. He is informing me there is a tumor at the base of my skull. It is all internal and pressing upon various nerves and tissues. He says, "We are not sure what it is, but suspect it is a very rare tumor (one in 10,000) which gives off epinephrine." (Epinephrine is a hormone like adrenalin that causes you to flee or fight. It could be the cause of my anxiety and short attention span!) The first thing I ask is, "What can be done?" Each doctor is mentioning that more tests are needed and they do not know if the tumor is operable. I am stunned, but somehow unexpectedly calmer for a few minutes. At least I know now that something real has been identified as the cause for my problems. I have a faint glimmer of hope that my mind and emotions can return to normal someday and all will be well. I also realize that if it is inoperable, I will certainly die!

Now, the neurosurgeon is speaking last, telling me regretfully that he does not have the skill to operate on this type of tumor and believes that no one in New Mexico would be capable of doing so. He hopes I can find someone, somewhere. I am shocked! He is standing up and walking toward the door. He is turning to look at me, nodding his head, somberly saying, "Good luck," as he hastily exits. My glimmer of hope diminishes to almost nothing. Dr. Abel is telling me there are more tests to take, to verify the tentative diagnosis and is assuring me she will look for someone to remove the tumor, if that is what I decide to do. Of course that is what I want to do. I know I have no choice! I want so much to live, but part of me well knows that I might die.

The next few days are filled with more tests and more drugs to stabilize my blood pressure. The diagnosis of my tumor has been verified. The technical name for it is pheochromocytoma. This kind of tumor is slow growing, and is usually benign.

I am so drugged from the Neurontin that I must struggle to stay awake and can only concentrate with great difficulty. I can no longer use any of my usual methods to heal myself. I am virtually helpless and in a constant state of anxiety that I will die. (I learn from one of the doctors that people with pheochromocytomas usually experience "feelings of doom" from the epinephrine in their blood stream.) Since I have been programmed from childhood to hide any illness, it takes courage to notify my family that something is terribly physically wrong with me. As I speak to my adult children by phone, I sense that they don't seem to know how to respond. I can hear shock in their voices. They have never seen me out of control. I feel somehow guilty for causing everyone so much trouble, but I know I have no choice. Brian notifies the Unity Church I attend and describes my situation to our minister. The minister and membership offer to help in any way they can.

After eight days in the hospital, I am discharged to go home until I either prepare to die or find a surgeon who will agree to try to remove the tumor. I discover that I cannot drive, as my reaction times are too slow and I even fear that I will fall asleep at the wheel. My symptoms are the result of all the drugs I must take for major pain and blood pressure control, in order to temporarily keep going.

Friends, church members, and Brian volunteer to take me wherever I need to go, and help me with anything I need. I am discovering who my real friends are. I am so thankful for the loving compassion and actual physical help from so many people. It is a new experience for me to be on the receiving end for help with a difficult situation. The genuine caring expressed by so many people touches my heart and brings tears to my eyes just to think of it.

However, not all of the people around me provide support. There are some neighbors with whom I thought I was developing a bond, who now avoid me, while perfect strangers at the church I have been attending for about a year, stand by me and volunteer to help me in any way they can. My friend Brian is also remaining by me at every juncture, even though we have only known each other for a few months. Since my family lives far away and are not easily available, many strangers have stepped in with great loving kindness to support me. I am unaccustomed to being the recipient of such loving care. It sometimes feels somewhat embarrassing as well as touches my heart. It is a constant reminder to me of the goodness within so many people. I am continuing to be deeply touched by their efforts and begin to realize that I am learning how to receive unsolicited loving kindness for the first time in my life.

Dr. Abel is searching for someone who will be willing to undertake the operation necessary to save my life. She has had great difficulty finding any physician who will even consider operating on my rare tumor. Finally, one day, after about two weeks of searching, she calls me and says, "I have found a neurosurgeon at Stanford University Medical Center in Palo Alto, California who has agreed to remove your tumor!"

I am so relieved, but I know that I must mentally and physically prepare myself to travel from Santa Fe to Palo Alto, while continuing to feel extremely anxious and frightened for my life. Dr. Abel suggests, "Put your affairs in order before you go, just in case."

CHAPTER 4

The Trauma Deepens

My mind is so addled that I am having difficulty handling my affairs. I am struggling to get my home in order and find someone to care for my beloved kitten, Maurice, while I will be gone. I am not even able to read my mail because of my inability to concentrate. My bills have started to pile up. It takes all the energy I have, to appear somewhat normal. Members of my church never flag in their efforts to help and continue to volunteer to drive me to appointments and help me shop for groceries. Brian is helping also. It is so difficult to appear fully present for others as I sometimes nod off during conversations, just as some old people do. Even though I am too ill to feel embarrassed most of the time, I still feel it occasionally. I wonder if I will ever have a normal life again, even if I live. One day is merging into the next. I am experiencing the profound realization that I cannot exist without the help of others. This harsh reality is so difficult for me to absorb that I feel so helpless and entirely out of control of my life. This is a traumatic experience for me! What is the meaning of it, I wonder.

Finally, a date is set for my surgery. At last, I know when I must be at Stanford. It is in early April, 2000. Brian kindly offers to go with me to help me through this ordeal. I accept. I am beginning to feel some hope, as I believe I might have a chance to be released from this bondage of drugs, pain, exhaustion, and confusion. (After my discharge from the hospital in Santa Fe, I began to notice that my speech had become slightly slurred and I had developed some problems swallowing that caused me to choke occasionally.) I believe that I must have the operation completed as soon as possible. I am so impatient and have a sense of urgency as I yearn for this whole drama to be ended, whatever the outcome. My adult children will be coming from the other side of the country to support me, when I arrive in Palo Alto. I need to see them and know they are there for me.

Brian and I are now flying to Palo Alto and I am surprisingly peaceful. This flight is smooth and uneventful. We are finally here and have rented a car to drive to Stanford University Medical Center. It is not too far from the airport. In fact, I can see the medical complex in the distance. I am feeling excited and hopeful that the end of my nightmare is within sight. Now Brian and I are walking down a long corridor toward the surgeon's office within the hospital. I want to run as fast as I can to get there. Brian gently reminds me, "Calm down." (I now don't remember actually being admitted to the surgical wing of the Stanford Medical Center.) I only know that I will have a pleasant private hospital room. I have finally reached the surgeon's office. The nurse is mentioning to me that the doctor needs a few more tests, one of which is an ultrasound. I hope I will have the surgery tomorrow. I want this whole experience to be over so I can go back to a normal life. The doctor, a kindly middle aged man, who I immediately like, is introducing himself. Now he is looking at all the tests and information that had been gathered in Santa Fe. He says, "I have ordered an ultrasound and will meet with you in your room, after the ultrasound, to discuss your surgery tomorrow." (An ultrasound is a noninvasive painless procedure using sound waves to penetrate your body that can define tumors or other internal structural abnormalities.) The ultrasound technician comes in and completes the test. It takes about a half hour and is painless. I feel so relieved to be here! The doctor returns to the ultrasound room and is motioning to an orderly that I am ready to be taken back to my room. As I am being wheeled back to my room, I am feeling so happy to have found such a kind surgeon.

It is evening, and the doctor has not yet come to see me. I am wondering why he is not here. My children will be here tomorrow. They will be here for my surgery. He has not come!

It is morning. My three children and Brian are here. I am filling out all the appropriate forms for my surgery. I am feeling sad because I have to fill out forms that ask questions such as: "What do want to do with your organs, if you do not survive?" "Do you want to be resuscitated if you are brain dead?" "Do you understand the risks involved in the surgery?" I am extremely sobered by this process. I am saddened by it, but also feel impatient and ready to get the whole experience over, so I can leave and be cured. Then suddenly, something unexpected happens!

A nurse is entering the room and is informing me that "The doctor you saw yesterday, who had been contacted by Dr. Abel, has refused to do your surgery, as it is more complicated than he had believed. He has transferred your case to Griffith Harsh MD, the head neurosurgeon at Stanford University Hospital at this time." The nurse also tells me that Dr. Harsh has agreed to take my case after looking at all the results of my tests. Another shock, as I realize that everything seems to have gone wrong but, at least I can feel thankful that someone will at least try to help me, and not leave me to die from my tumor. I know in my heart that Dr. Harsh is my last and only hope. I wonder if he will operate on me today.

Dr. Harsh, a man who exudes power and knowledge from his very presence, suddenly strides into my hospital room followed by a large entourage of interns, residents, medical students, nurses, and a few other curious doctors. He does not mince his words and briskly informs me. "Your tumor is wrapped around your carotid artery, and it is possible, if you survive the surgery, that you will be without this artery on your left side. This can cause brain damage." He adds, "You might lose your voice and ability to swallow. I might have to cut nerves that will cause deafness in your left ear, and you will most certainly lose a nerve to a muscle in your back. I must cut the vagus nerve on one side of your body to remove the tumor." (The vagus nerve controls balance, digestion, heart function, swallowing, and various glandular functions. It is the tenth cranial nerve and is connected to the vocal cords.) Dr. Harsh then says calmly, "You have a fifty-fifty chance of surviving the surgery." My mind involuntarily again begins to wander as I feel driven to think even more concretely about my possible death. I wonder what death will be like and again, if I have completed my mission during this lifetime. I wonder what the meaning of my life has been. Thoughts of my childhood again continue to intrude upon my awareness as I think back to the first time I encountered death and remember what I learned. As I relive this encounter from my past, I am surprised by my strong emotion.

Encounter with Death

I was thirteen years old. My father was a role model for me. We were closely bonded and often shared many deep discussions. I loved him dearly.

One morning, while I was in bed sleeping, my mother came into my room and shook me awake. She sat on my bed and began to cry, and tearfully told me: "Your father is dying." I remember holding her and comforting her. She told me that my father was in their bedroom and had experienced a stroke during the night. My mother described his paralysis which was on one side of his body, and told me that the doctor had been there while I slept. She then said, "You must go into his bedroom and give him a hug." I remember the fear I felt as I walked down the hall to their bedroom. When I first saw him, I peeked around the doorway and was somewhat shocked at what I saw. I felt so helpless and feared that I wouldn't know how to help and what to do.

My father was lying in his bed, breathing heavily. As he looked at me, I could see that his mouth was drawn to one side and one eye was partially closed. He could not talk, only make groaning noises. I somehow understood what it was all about, and suddenly felt great compassion and love for him. I ran into his arms, and remember that he was only able to embrace me with one arm. I knew his mind was fully present and felt powerless to help him. My mother told me he could not eat or drink and was "going to die." I experienced a deep sadness in my chest and suppressed a scream that threatened to erupt from my throat. I had never experienced grief like this before.

The next few days were somewhat of a blur. My mother needed to go to the airport to pick up one of my three half-sisters who had begun their travels to our home in Ohio. I knew how important it was for me to help. I was left alone with my father for about an hour when my mother went to the airport. She had plans to pick up my half-sister and stop at the grocery store to get food for everyone. There was no one else in our home during that hour.

My father was still in his bed and my mother asked me to be there if he needed me, and to stay at his bedside. She said he could have a little water that must be dripped into his mouth from a fork. After she left, I lay down on the twin bed next to him and began to watch him breathe. (I felt a little scared and yet proud that I was trusted with such an important responsibility. I hoped he wouldn't die while I was alone with him. My mother had not told me what to do if that happened.)

He seemed to be sleeping and was breathing deeply with his eyes closed. Suddenly he opened his eyes and tried to speak to me. I couldn't understand him. It just sounded like mumbling. Then, with his good hand, he grasped my hand and guided it to the fork that was in a glass of water on his bedside stand. I understood him and will never forget the look of gratitude on his face as he communicated his wishes to me. He looked both loving and desperate. I took the fork and put drop after drop of water into his mouth until he was satisfied. I felt so close to him. He looked at me intently and lovingly once more and then closed his eyes, as he again seemed to drift off to sleep. I remember the tears rolling down my face. This was to be our last connection. I never connected with him heart-to-heart again. It was profound and very emotional for me. About an hour after I gave him the water, he went into a coma and died the next day. I was grief stricken and did not yet understand that I had precipitously left childhood forever.

My life was never the same after that. I still knew I wanted to be a doctor, like my father, and I felt grief as well as a sense of pride in being able to help him. It gave me comfort to feel that sense of closeness to him that I experienced before he died. I now knew what death really meant and wondered where his spirit had gone. I hoped he was still watching over me. There was a small part of me that was angry at him for dying and leaving me. That part of me felt fatherless and abandoned. My father had taught me about caring for others, helping others, and trying to live a life that would leave the world a better place. In this, I was all alone. My mother needed me to take care of her, and I did.

Dr. Harsh's crisp voice is drawing me back to the here and now in Stanford. I am well aware that he wants me to fully understand the worst possible scenario in the surgery that will be performed. I want to know all of the possibilities and deal with all of them, but I feel emotionally shaken repeatedly, as I absorb his description of what can happen. It is difficult to wrap my mind around the idea that I can become so handicapped. I, who present workshops around the world and consider myself to have a powerful speaking voice, cannot fathom the possibility of being unable to speak loudly. Dr. Harsh says I will still have one vocal cord, but will never be able to speak loudly again. He also informs me that I could lose one carotid artery.

There are two carotid arteries in the neck. They are next to the jugular veins. The carotids are large blood vessels that supply blood to the large front part of the brain. This is where thinking, speech, personality and sensory and motor functions reside. You can feel your pulse in the carotid arteries on each side of your neck, right below the angle of the jaw line.

Still, I know that I have no choice but to go forward with the surgery. It is the surgery or death—and I don't want to die. There are so many things I still want to do with my life. I am ready.

Then, yet another shock is delivered by Dr. Harsh. He says sternly "You cannot have the surgery for four weeks." His reasoning is that a team of doctors must be organized to deal with my situation. One of the team members, an anesthesiologist who has helped remove this type of tumor many times, is presently in Africa. Anesthesia is critical to success of the procedure as removal of a pheochromocytoma can either cause a surge of epinephrine that can kill a patient with a stroke or heart attack or a sudden withdrawal of epinephrine that will cause a patient to go into cardiac arrest. Dr. Harsh reiterates that it is critical that I have a team of surgeons and also informs me that my surgery will take between twelve and fifteen hours.

I begin to lose control of my feelings after hearing all this. I feel tears rolling down my face. I cry "How can this be? How can I go back to New Mexico after making all the arrangements for my family as well as myself here in Palo Alto?" I feel like finally, "the bottom has fallen out." What about my family who have travelled so far? I cry and I cry. Dr. Harsh explains to the interns, residents, nurses, and physicians present that my loss of emotional control is because of epinephrine from the tumor that is causing my anxiety. He then turns and walks away, followed by his medical entourage. I realize there is nothing to negotiate.

I just want the surgery to be over as soon as possible. The stress of waiting feels overwhelming. I am so helpless. I can sense that my adult children are not pleased either, but they are saying that they will come back to support me when I return for the surgery. My friend Brian continues to be very supportive and says that he will bring me back to Palo Alto when the surgery is rescheduled as well as stay with me until it is completed. I am so thankful for the support of my children and Brian.

There are more tests, and I am going to be sent home to Santa Fe, with what seems like a huge blood pressure monitor that can take my blood pressure at night while I sleep. It weighs about fifteen pounds and measures twelve by sixteen inches. I am instructed to take my blood pressure every two hours while awake and was prescribed even more drugs to take, both alpha blockers and beta blockers. I am expected to become more stabilized during the month. I feel miserable and so alone. I wonder if I should have moved closer to my children, instead of to Santa Fe.

It is now the night before I must go back to Santa Fe. I think it is about 8:00 p.m. and dark outside. I am feeling so frightened about all that has transpired. My hospital room door opens and a nurse is entering. She is coming up to my bedside with a serious look on her face. I am wondering "what now?" I notice that her eyes look sad. She says, "I want to talk with you about what you should do." When I ask what she wants to tell me, she states, "I think you should go home, put your things in order and make the best of the time you have left! Your chances of survival are slim, and if you do, life could be horrible."

Hearing this is very upsetting. She has verbalized my worst fears. I feel a knot in the pit of my stomach and tears again come to my eyes. I believe she is a knowledgeable health care practitioner and see the sorrow on her face, as she shares her thoughts. She has given up the idea that I have any chance for survival with a good life. I notice this sadness in others' eyes also, but try to disregard it. I realize now, that I am an object of pity, another totally new experience for me. I, of course, reject her recommendations and know with more intensity than ever, that I must do everything I can to survive and have a good life. I begin to think of alternative things I can do to help myself survive. I am again reminded that since I cannot concentrate well enough, I will not be able to use any of the alternative techniques I learned over the years to help myself, except mindfulness.

CHAPTER 5
The Preparation

It is the day after my aborted surgery, and I am flying back to Santa Fe with Brian. My days are filled with total self-absorption. I accept all the help that others have offered, to prepare me for the surgery. The helplessness of my situation has caused me to become totally self-centered. This emotional state continues to feel like a strange and new experience, but my guilt over being such a bother is outweighed by my sheer terror and neediness. I continue to experience myself as a time bomb, ready to explode.

I am trying everything in alternative medicine I can think of that does not require much concentration. These methods include acupuncture, Dahn Yoga, Energy Medicine, and counseling. I am still unable to concentrate, but want to remove any possible impediment to my survival. Since I cannot drive, members from my church volunteer to take me to appointments and are continuing to shop for me. My friend Brian also continues to be a major support, helping me with my busy schedule, as well as taking me out for an occasional movie or dinner to distract my mind from my present dilemma. Most importantly, he offers emotional support.

My blood pressure is stabilizing at around 195/100. (This is still within the danger zone.) I'm having difficulty concentrating for more than a few minutes and still find myself falling asleep during conversations. This is troubling as I do not want to identify with the old people I have seen doing this. I do not like myself very much and am somewhat astounded that anyone wants to be around me at all. Days again melt into one another. Every day when I wake up, I am a little startled to realize that I am still alive.

One day I decide to do something daring. I have always watched people speeding by on motorcycles, but I am fearful of riding them as I believe they are extremely dangerous. Brian invited me to ride on his motorcycle several times, and I declined. However, with death staring me in the face, I decide to finally accept his invitation. I believe if I am going to die anyway, I want to leave this life, having had a motorcycle experience. I tell Brian I am finally ready to take a motorcycle ride and would like to do it now. I realize that I have been living my life within a myth, my own personal myth that I am invincible.

Brian is smiling and nodding, as we go out to his motorcycle, which is parked in front of my house. He is handing me a helmet and making sure I am dressed properly for the ride. Now he shows me how to get on his motorcycle, and where to hold on. I'm climbing up behind him and holding on tightly. Brian revs up his motorcycle and begins our short ride, with me hanging on the back and holding on for dear life. I must be careful to hold on to him and lean as he does. Even though I am wondering if I will survive this ride, I am less fearful than I ever imagined I could be. I am actually enjoying the feelings of freedom and closeness to nature as the wind whistles by! The ride is over and I am still alive! I feel a deep satisfaction from my accomplishment. If I can do this, I think perhaps, I can also survive the surgery.

Finally, it is the night before I am scheduled to go back to Palo Alto. As I lie in my bed waiting for sleep, many thoughts float through my head. Even though I am drugged, I am still terrified. I am now not only afraid I will die, but am simultaneously afraid I will live, but with brain damage or some other major impediment. I think about dying and wonder again if I have completed my mission in life. I know I have helped a lot of people, but it still does not feel complete. There is so much more I want to accomplish, but I am not clear on what it is, or if I will be able to do it. I again think about my past and how I have been guided in some unseen way to continue to pursue many unusual treatment modalities. I also start to think again about God. I am able to say a few prayers and believe I can feel prayers of the many others praying for me. I am wondering if there really is life after death. As I drift off to sleep, I remember something that happened when I was three years old.

A Past Life Experience?

I was three years old and believed that I could remember many things as far back as before my birth. My mother had just tucked me in bed for the night and I decided I would tell her about what I remembered. I had been wondering for a long time about where I was at the time these things happened. I remember telling her about everything in detail and then saying, "Where was I when those things happened?" I recall how she seemed to listen thoughtfully and then paused for a few minutes. I could hardly wait for her answer! Now I could find out, as I believed my mother knew everything. She said, "You were in heaven." I accepted her response immediately and then dismissed it from my mind. It seemed logical.

My last thoughts, right before sleep, are of hope, that if I should die, perhaps I will be reincarnated. This memory fills me with peace. I don't have to accomplish everything in this lifetime. I am thinking about many reports of reincarnation, mediumship, out-of-body experiences, and channeling, that I believe present evidence of life after death.

Life after Death

Stephen Braude pursued the question of existence after death. His 2003 book, *Immortal Remains, The Evidence for Life after Death,* explored research involving cases of mediumship, channeling, reincarnation, possession, out-of-body experiences, near-death experiences, hauntings, and transplant cases. He concluded that there is evidence for life after death. I find this is very reassuring to me.

The experience when I was three years old that involved the memory of a past life as well as an out-of-body experience at age eighteen comforted me as well as validated my life long hypothesis that there was life after death. I have never deviated from belief in that probability.

When I was initially being trained as a clinical psychologist, we were taught that we must not bring up anything spiritual with our patients. So, I conscientiously avoided working with spiritual issues for years, even though at times I was tempted to discuss something spiritual with certain clients. Over these years, my clients finally taught me that they sometimes desperately needed to speak of their various religious perceptions and conflicts. I decided it was important to address their needs, and did so, being careful not to insinuate any of my beliefs upon them. Over the last ten years, the psychological community has done an about face, and now recommends spiritual issues can and should be addressed in therapy.

A patient I shall call Anne volunteered, early in therapy, that she had a strong belief in God and perceived Him as judging her as damaged and dirty because of all the sexual abuses she had endured.

Anne believed she would go to hell after death because of what had happened to her. Child abuse victims usually blame themselves for what happened to them, as it gives them more of a sense of control. They often believe that if it is their fault, all they must do is to refrain from whatever they were doing that was wrong.

Anne made great strides in therapy during the first several months, but continued to experience deep feelings of worthlessness, stemming from her perceptions about God's feelings toward her. She described to me how she visualized God. To her he looked like a kindly old man.

I decided to use guided imagery with her and, with her permission, helped her visualize herself as an infant in the arms of her kindly God, before she was born. She was able to visualize well, and for the first time in her memory could actually feel the love of God filling her mind and body as her God was reassuring her that the abuse she would experience as a child after her birth would not be her fault, and that he would always love her. (These visualizations were constructed to fit her perceptions of God.)

After her guided imagery session, Anne reported that she felt very relieved. Her anxiety related to work became minimal. A month later she was able to return to work and never had another panic attack. She continued to make rapid progress in therapy, which she completed in six months. Anne's case is an example of the importance of exploring spiritual beliefs when dealing with deep seated fears of death.

Deepak Chopra in his book, *God: A Story of Revelation,* supports the proposition that there are actual neural mechanisms for spirituality. Chopra believes that different levels of consciousness affect how we may experience God. He looks back at various visionaries who were eager for God and describes the four paths open to them to reach a higher level of consciousness.

The first path is the path of *devotion*. It utilizes much prayer and an immersion in wonder before God and all divine works. The poet Rumi exemplified this path. Individuals on this path have been described as having a "love affair" with the divine.

The second path is the path of *understanding*. This is a more cognitive path and involves reflecting on the great question of life such as: Who am I? Why was I created? What is my purpose in life? This is the path Socrates took, as a scholar and philosopher. The mind can actually cause the searcher to become as much or more passionate about God as those on the path of devotion.

The third path is the path of *service*. It involves giving yourself selflessly to others. The actions of devotees on this path, draws them closer to God by identifying with God by the act of giving with no rewards.

The fourth path is the path of *meditation*. It is a path to enhance consciousness. Devotees practice deep meditation, which opens their mind to higher levels of consciousness deep within their very essence, enabling them to feel more deeply connected to God.

As I considered all these paths, I realized that my path has been twofold: primarily the path of service intermingled with the path of understanding.

But now, because I think I might die, I am also continuing to examine my mission in life and whether or not I have accomplished it. I consider the quote from Buddha: "When you die, only three things matter; how much you have loved, how gently you have lived, and how gracefully you have let go of things not meant for you." These thoughts comfort me.

CHAPTER 6
Closer to The Door of Death

I am again on a plane with Brian, flying to Palo Alto. The flight is uneventful, and I am, of course, dreading as well as looking forward to the experience of my upcoming surgery. I can feel anxiety in the pit of my stomach and bands of tightness across my chest. I am so glad my friend Brian is with me. I am not sure if I could survive this trip alone and my level of dependency upon him surprises me. I do not enjoy being so dependent. I have been feeling so much weaker and more helpless every day.

We rented a car again, and Brian is driving to Stanford Medical Center for the second time. I am admitted to the hospital quickly.

Even though I believe that I am psychologically ready for the surgery to be done immediately, the medical team wants even more diagnostic tests before the surgery. A nurse is telling, me, "They didn't do these tests earlier when you were here the first time, as they were not sure you would survive the month." I was unprepared for the test that followed.

This most important test demands that I remain conscious during a torturous procedure! The medical team needs to determine if I can live without one carotid artery. I will need to be conscious while they block my carotid artery, so they can determine the effects of its loss upon my brain, in case they need to remove the artery during my surgery. They will make an incision in my groin and thread a catheter through the artery passing through my abdomen, into and through my heart, and beyond, up to my left carotid artery which is located in my neck. (A catheter is a flexible rubber tube that is small enough to travel through the arteries and will be pushed through them.)

Even though they have given me another drug to further relieve my anxiety, I am still feeling terrified. I fully understand the procedure, as I am a nurse. This causes me to feel more agitated than someone who may not fully understand all the dangers. I am silently praying that I will live through this test. I know I must endure the procedure, with the knowledge that at any moment something can go wrong, and I can die.

The doctors are now beginning: first injecting Novacain into my groin, then making an incision. All I can feel is a sense of pressure. I am surprised that there is no pain. The doctor is informing me, "Now we are going through your abdomen." I can actually physically feel pressure where the catheter is being guided. It is terrifying to me, as I am visualizing the whole process as well as where the arteries are located. Several minutes later, he informs me, "Now we are going into your heart." I am in terror in spite of the tranquilizer and believe my heart skips several beats! It seems like immediately after he informed me the catheter was entering my heart, he is now saying in a gentle tone, "Now it is leaving your heart and will soon be arriving at your carotid artery." I am becoming breathless and wish I could leave my body.

I now hear the doctor saying as if in the distance, "We are now going to block your carotid artery and will talk with you so we can determine if you can manage without this carotid artery." I am able to speak, but almost immediately forget what I am saying. The next thing I remember is someone telling me that the test was, "completed without incident." I am left feeling somehow violated. The attendants wheel me back to my room, where I must lie quietly for several hours, to avoid a hemorrhage. As I look up at the ceiling, I decide to allow myself to cry quietly. I feel as if I have been to hell and back.

Two resident doctors are walking into my room and one is telling me that they have determined that "You will probably live even if we have to remove your carotid artery. However, we are not sure how doing that would affect your mind. Do you have any questions?" I have none. This experience has been extremely terrifying and traumatizing to me in my weakened, drugged state.

After the test and the resident's explanation that I could live without a carotid artery, I find myself alone and crying again with even deeper feelings of helplessness and growing awareness of the total lack of control of my life. Everything I have taken for granted has been shattered, destroyed by the weight of the many physical assaults that have happened to me since that fateful day when I bought my blood pressure monitor. Suddenly Dr. Harsh enters and says, "Tomorrow morning we will operate on you." As I begin to drift off to sleep, I begin to think again about God.

How God changes Your Brain

Newberg and Newman in their seminal book, *How God Changes Your Brain,* report that they have discovered there are neural mechanisms in place for spirituality. It does not matter which religion the person accepts. This book does not tell you if God exists, but its authors explain that religious beliefs enhance neural functioning of the brain in ways that improve physical and emotional health. They also discovered that each part of the brain constructs different perceptions of God and that every human being assembles his or her perception of God in uniquely different ways, that give God different shades of meaning and value for each person.

Various spiritual practices and religious beliefs enhance neural function in ways that improve physical and emotional health. If the practices are intense and long term, they appear to permanently change the structure of those parts of the brain that control mood and give rise to more conscious notions of self. They may actually shape our sensory perception of the world. These practices strengthen specific neurological circuits that generate peacefulness, social awareness, and compassion for others.

From a neurological perspective, God is a perception and experience that is constantly changing within each individual. They also discovered that spiritual practices like meditation and prayer help as well, even if the person practicing them is an atheist.

Atheism is also a spiritual path, as much as any other spiritual belief system. Patients whose path is atheism need equal support during their journeys. I've worked with a number of atheistic patients who needed to explore the meaning of death from that perspective. It is important to make that help available to all patients facing death, not only in hospital settings, but after the patient returns home. I know that I am fortunate to have the help of my minister, both now and after my surgery when I return home, if I should survive. I know I will have need for this kind of help. If I survive this journey, I am determined that I will be able to integrate and reconfigure my life.

Surgery

The day dawns with light rays silently slipping through the windows of my room. It is about 6:00 a.m. I feel strangely disconnected and actually peaceful on this day. I know I have done everything I can to prepare. My daughter Karen and friend Brian are not here yet, but should arrive soon. They give me great comfort as I know I am not physically alone. I have done everything I can to survive, and am aware in the very core of my being that everything is out of my hands. It is up to the doctors, nurses and God. It helps to know that many people are praying for me.

Feeling a Presence

Suddenly I feel a warm glow flow through my body and experience a strange sensation around my heart. It is as though someone or something is caressing my heart! I am experiencing an absolute oneness with all living things. Love is surrounding me, flowing through me, and enveloping me with its warmth. I see a gentle light in the room and am transfixed by my knowing! Tears of joy are flowing down my cheeks.

I know with every cell in my mind and my body that love, empathy, and forgiveness are the ultimate and highest goals to which human beings can aspire. The salvation of man is through these three things. I know without doubt the invisible energy that some healers are able to access comes from this field of love. I am actually experiencing within myself total oneness with all living things for the first time in my life. I know that I will never be alone again. I am part of this field of oneness that is like a sea of love and knowledge of everything and everyone. My heart feels as though it is opening wider and I now feel empathy with all people, and all living things in the world.

As this field of love and oneness envelops me, I think about all the different kinds of love I know about and have studied. I know about romantic love, filial love for one's brothers and sisters, maternal love, and agape love for all human beings.

The field of love I am experiencing expands far beyond that. It includes empathy with all. Empathy is the ability to actually experience as well as understand the feelings of others. One can love and sympathize with others, but not experience their feelings. In order to have close connection with, and fully understand another, one must have empathy. I know this as a truth.

While in this loving state, I also observe myself becoming very philosophical for a few moments. I clearly know that Descartes' statement: "I think, therefore, I am" is only a beginning truth related to consciousness.

A more evolved philosophical statement that comes from a part of my mind right now regarding consciousness is: "I think, therefore I know I exist and I love, therefore I can know who I am."

I feel great peace as I am filled with this love, but for some reason I do not understand, I still refrain from praying for myself today, even though I believe in prayer and know of its positive effects upon people. I can easily pray for others, but it is more difficult to pray for my own survival. It seems unnecessary. I wonder if perhaps it is because I know all is well and God surrounds me.

My work with various healers around the world and studies of the research of Larry Dossey and others about the effects of prayer, convinced me of its value a number of years ago. Now, I actually experience and know without doubt that both positive and negative thoughts have the power to affect the human body. I'm suddenly pulled out of this peaceful reverie by a sound.

I hear the sound of the wheels of a stretcher coming down the hall. I wonder if it is for me. This possibility intrigues me and I am not afraid. It is for me!

Karen and Brian are also now in the doorway of my room, waiting in the hall. Within a minute two orderlies enter my room and help me slide onto the stretcher to begin my trip down the hall to the surgical wing of the hospital. I am wondering what I will experience. As the stretcher is rolled down the hallway to the surgical suite, I note the lights in the ceiling and think of all the cases of near-death experience that people have reported, about going to a place of light and love; or seeing themselves outside of their body. I hope it will be positive for me, like that. I also think of all the people I have loved, who have died, and wonder if they will be nearby to help me, if I die during my surgery. I am aware of the continuing comfort from that possibility, as well as the actual awareness that many people are praying for me now.

I am now saying goodbye to Karen and Brian who have been walking next to my stretcher as I am traversing the hallway. I feel alone and, at the same time, surrounded by love.

The electric doors at the entrance to the operating suite open, and I am finally being wheeled into the operating room, feeling physically alone, but still emotionally connected to that field of love, empathy, and forgiveness, as well as oneness with the people who are praying for me. I wonder what I will experience.

The operating room is so cold. I'm shivering! I hope I won't get chilled. I am startled by the cold. It feels so impersonal in this room. Various doctors and nurses are bustling around, tending to their different tasks. There are so many masked people. No one seems focused on me at all. Now, I think I see Dr. Harsh. He peers at me over his mask and is quickly walking over to me, identifying himself. He says "Are you ready?" I answer, "More than ready." He tells me that he is ready and will be with me until the surgery is over. I say, "Yes, please take good care of me!" That is the last thing I remember before losing consciousness.

CHAPTER 7

Survival

The next thing I remember is waking up in intensive care three days after surgery. My daughter Karen is here, as is Brian. I feel their concern and am aware, with some relief that I can still talk. However, I am only able to speak in a breathless whisper and cannot swallow without choking. I experience a sense of constant panic. I am propped up in bed on many pillows and am not allowed to attempt to stand up. Karen tells me "You have really been out of it, Mom." She and Brian both tell me that I had said, "The doctors are trying to kill me." I do not remember any of this, but am relieved that the surgery is over, and that I am still alive. They tell me that the surgery took thirteen-and-a-half hours.

I don't want them to leave my side, as I realize I am terrified of being alone for even a few minutes. I have the sensation that I will choke and die, if I am left alone. I know that my emotions are out of my control and I suddenly realize at the same time that my head and neck are swathed in heavy bandages. Karen tells me that I was so anxious, that the doctors administered the tranquilizer, Ativan. After receiving the Ativan, Karen says, "I thought you were having hallucinations and asked the staff not to give it to you anymore." I feel embarrassed about how I must have behaved, even though I don't remember it. Brian is mentioning that my head and neck had been swollen to about three times normal size, but says that most of the swelling has gone down. I feel guilty for what I am putting everyone through, and wonder how anyone can bear to be around me with all my tubes and my distorted face. I have always felt it important to look attractive in every situation. My mindful self knows this is impossible. Any vanity I had left is now gone. I know clearly that vanity is the last thing that matters, even though I am saddened by its departure.

Now, thankfully, I have a sense that my mind is fully present, but for some reason, I still feel anxious. I believe I cannot trust any of the doctors or nurses. Since I know how to use the technique of mindfulness, I wonder why I do not trust anyone and feel so anxious.

My mindful self diagnoses me as paranoid and I am aware that my anxiety and mistrust are detrimental to my healing. However, I cannot control these thoughts and feelings, even though I try. I can only observe them. I also begin to consider the possibility that I might have Post Traumatic Stress Disorder(PTSD). I yearn to experience that calm sense of incredible oneness I experienced right before my surgery.

Post Traumatic Stress Disorder

I am extremely familiar from my work with my patients, of the disorder called PTSD. I realize that I am now beginning to think about other people; this feels like progress. The following is a list of what is needed to qualify for the diagnosis of PTSD.

THE EVENT: There must be an identified event that provides the experience of threatened death, serious injury or sexual violence. In order to qualify as a traumatic event, the situation may occur by directly experiencing the event, or even possibly witnessing the event as it happened to someone else or, learning that the event occurred to a close family member or friend. In some cases, experiencing repeated or extreme exposure to aversive details of the event can qualify as sufficiently traumatizing. (Years ago I worked with a court reporter who had been traumatized by hearing and transcribing the details of horror that had been described in a murder case.)

That case involved an infamous serial killer who murdered young homosexual men and stored their body parts in his freezer. Details of his actions before, during, and after his murders were horrifying and almost unbelievable. All those who heard them felt traumatized by visualizing what he had done. This case was heard in Milwaukee, Wisconsin. The prisoner's name was Jeffrey Dahmer.

I am aware that I experienced numerous traumatic health events, followed by a traumatic diagnosis and other treatment modalities while in the hospital.

The first traumatic event was when the hospital staff in the emergency room could not get my blood pressure down and I began to think I might not survive. The second event was the first time I was told my diagnosis and the probability that my tumor might be inoperable. The third significant event was being sent back from Palo Alto when the surgery was postponed. The fourth was my heart catheterization, when I felt violated and feared death during the whole procedure.

THE INTRUSIONS: Intrusions are considered to be some of the symptoms of PTSD. They may include the intrusion of distressing memories of the event, flashbacks, dreams about the event, loss of awareness of present surroundings and distress when exposed to things that recall the event. Patients often report some of these symptoms after medical and physical trauma. I often avoided things that reminded me of my suffering. I found it difficult to watch movies or TV programs that reminded me of what had occurred. For about six months after the surgery, I sometimes had periods of remembering those traumatic events when I was occupied with life in the here and now. Writing this book caused me to re-experience many of the past traumas.

AVOIDANCE: Avoidance of anything that might remind one of the traumatic event is also a common after-effect from experiencing the traumatic event. An individual may make efforts to avoid the thoughts or feelings, activities or situations that are reminders of what had occurred. Victims of trauma may even deal with their pain by repressing memories of the trauma. Sometimes their efforts to avoid reminders of the traumatic events take so much mental energy that they experience diminished interest in normal life activities and experience feelings of detachment or estrangement as well as a restricted range of feelings, and a sense of a shortened future. Patients subconsciously often avoid the discomfort of remembering medical and physical trauma. As I mentioned earlier, for several years after the medical trauma, I could not watch TV shows or see movies about emergency medicine. Emergency room shows were totally off limits. Violence in any form was extremely upsetting to me.

AROUSAL: Other symptoms of PTSD may include symptoms of hyperarousal. Symptoms of hyperarousal include difficulty falling or staying asleep, irritability, outbursts of anger, difficulty concentrating, hypervigilance, exaggerated startle response, and general physiological over-reactivity. Hypervigilance may be described as always being prepared for something life threatening to happen. Sometimes individuals experiencing hypervigilance find it necessary to sit with their back to the wall so they can be ready to fight or flee should anything threaten them. For several years after my surgery, I had difficulty falling and staying asleep. Physiological over-reactivity was present. I felt a fear of death I had never experienced before.

Traumatized patients often report many of these symptoms. If they are unaware that they may have PTSD, they could remain trapped in the pain of their experiences and never recover emotionally from their trauma. I believed that I fulfilled the criteria for a PTSD diagnosis.

Patients who have PTSD as a result of a medical crisis can greatly benefit from some of the psychological treatments available today. They are the same treatments I have used with war veterans when they returned from battle with PTSD. These treatments are extremely effective and noninvasive.

NEGATIVE CHANGES IN MOOD OR THINKING: These symptoms are also sometimes found in victims of PTSD: They may include inordinate fears such as fear of death or loss of a loved one. After my life-saving surgery, I continued to experience almost constant fear of death for over a year.

DURATION: Duration of the symptoms of at least a month or more after the trauma is necessary to determine if the symptoms are a normal reaction to the trauma and will recover over a short period of time. My symptoms certainly lasted more than a month.

IMPAIRMENT: In order to fulfill the diagnosis of PTSD, symptoms such as negative changes in mood or thinking, hyperarousal, avoidance, and intrusions that follow an identified traumatic event must cause significant impairment to social, occupational, or other important areas of functioning. Many patients who have experienced significant medical trauma may have been affected in ways that limit their social and occupational functioning. I felt unable to go back to work for two months and extremely dependent upon others emotionally for at least six months after my surgery.

The treatment of PTSD has evolved tremendously in the past twenty years. Psychological treatment is highly effective and can help severely traumatized patients recover and lead full lives.

It is important for both patients and therapists to define the meanings of the trauma that has been experienced. Trauma as well as loss, grief, and helplessness all cause inevitable suffering. Knowing this may not make the pain of one's suffering less, but at some point in the recovery process, may help patients open their minds and increase their ability to assess the meaning in their pain. (My body had never placed me in a physically critical situation in the past.)

Medical Treatment as a Cause of PTSD

There are three phases for routine hospital admission and treatment. Opportunities for debilitating traumatic events may occur in any or all three phases.

<u>The Admission Phase:</u> With admission to a hospital, either planned or unplanned, events that occur can be perceived by a patient as an infringement upon his or her body and psyche. What is traumatic for one individual may not be so for another. A person's past experience, age, sex, personality, and genetic make up are factors in their perception of trauma. The infringement on the body often eliminates privacy, which alone in itself could be traumatic to some individuals. An intravenous feeding tube (IV) is almost immediately inserted in the patient's arm, followed by tests of various kinds. Blood is invariably drawn for analysis and x-rays, and scans may be included. Questions that may not directly relate to a physical problem are asked, such as, Do you feel safe at home? Does anyone abuse you? Are you depressed? How often do you drink alcohol? These questions, important to medical staff, may feel invasive to many people. In addition, modesty may be challenged due to repetitive physical exams by different medical personnel.

If the hospitalization is due to an emergency, as mine was, the initial hospitalization may be more emotionally traumatic, causing feelings of fear, helplessness, and shock. Confusion from the speed of change in the patient's life situation is, in itself, traumatizing. These aspects of the admission phase may be great enough to cause symptoms of PTSD. My experience of the first phase was traumatic in part, because I knew too much. I was shocked by what I can best describe as my body's betrayal.

<u>The Treatment Phase</u>: After diagnosis, the patient may be treated by medical professionals with drugs; major surgery such as heart surgery or brain surgery; minor surgery such as an appendectomy, chemotherapy, psychotherapy, physical therapy, art therapy, or rehabilitation, to name only a few.

Treatment in itself can be extremely traumatizing, depending on the pain involved, recuperation necessary, medications needed and the level of threat of death or residual handicaps resulting from physical or emotional damage. (Some of the tests I experienced as well as the events related to my surgery were traumatizing emotionally as well as physically.)

<u>The Discharge Phase</u>: After discharge the patient must cope with recuperation and adjustment to life outside the hospital. This could be uneventful or filled with further traumatic experiences. This is the period when, right after my surgery, I felt relieved but still had to adjust to the handicap of a changed voice while recovering from the trauma of my previous diagnosis and treatment. I was still recovering from all the medications I had received as well as learning to walk more than a few steps without fainting.

Because I continued to feel somewhat out of control of my emotions I also noticed that I had a strange sensitivity to light and sound that was totally new to me. I could not tolerate watching TV, and could only listen to music at a low volume. I realized I was still totally dependent upon others to continue living, even though I didn't trust all my caregivers. I knew this was irrational, but I felt somehow as though I had been tortured, and was now under the control of my torturers. Fortunately, I did not have these feelings towards friends and family. I believed that I could trust them. My mindful self did trust my caregivers and knew that my lack of trust at another level was irrational.

Since I had always experienced myself as feeling emotionally solid and clear, I realized that I had never before been in the position of being the care "receiver," but had always been the care "giver." The situation in which I found myself then was perhaps more unacceptable to me than it would have been if I had been accustomed to accepting help from others. I felt as if I were waking up inside a nightmare that seemed never ending.

Analysis of the extreme anxiety, sensitivity to light, and paranoia, similar to that which I had experienced after my surgery, is found to be a common occurrence for patients who have been in an intensive care setting for long periods of time and may have been abruptly removed from the drug Neurontin. I was amazed and reassured to discover this fact. A stay in intensive care itself can leave one as traumatized as going to war.

As many as one out of three people who spend several days in intensive care, experience nightmares, depression, and hallucinations. Patients are often well prepared for the physical aftermath of their procedures, but can be totally unprepared for the emotional effects of intensive care.

I discovered that rapid withdrawal from Neurontin usually results in bizarre side effects. The described side effects matched what I had been experiencing. A blog on the internet described these symptoms. Things were beginning to make more sense.

An article dated 5/15/15 from Pfizer, the company who originally manufactured Neurontin, stated that Neurontin can cause serious side effects if withdrawn abruptly. These may include: thoughts about suicide or dying, attempt to commit suicide, new or worse depression, new or worse anxiety, feeling agitated or restless, panic attacks, insomnia, new or worse irritability, aggressiveness, being angry or violent, acting on dangerous impulses, extreme increase in activity and talking, and other unusual changes in behavior or mood. (Pfizer Medical Information-USA 5/15/15) Even though I went through the trauma of my experience with drug withdrawal problems, I note it here with the hope of possibly preventing this type of error happening to others. This drug was necessary to alleviate my pain, but the pharmaceutical company did not warn the medical community at the time of my surgery of the probable side effects of rapid withdrawal.

The Four-Bed Ward

I have now been fully conscious for one day and am being wheeled from intensive care to a four bed ward next to the nursing station. I am so glad to be leaving intensive care. It is so confusing to have lights on all the time. The nurse tells me that all the other patients in my new room have just had brain surgery and are in various stages of recovery. My surgery was in my neck; thus, I am fully conscious and aware. I notice that all the beds have curtains around them and ask the nurse to please pull back my curtains, so I can see the window and natural light coming in. The nurse insists that I must have the curtains around my bed at all times for privacy. I want to see and talk with my fellow patients and can tell from the voices in the room that there are both male and female patients present. I am beginning to feel myself becoming somewhat confused. The white curtains are around all the beds. I believe the isolation created by the curtains is adding to my confusion. I hear strange noises coming from the other patients in the room and don't know what they mean. There are many moans and groans as well as a few screams. I don't know what is happening and I am scared. I have no way to check reality. My imagination seems like it is going wild. I feel so helpless.

It is now the second night and I am beginning to relax for the night. The curtains around my bed are suddenly yanked open, and a woman with her head swathed in bandages and a look of terror on her face leans over me and lets out a loud rasping scream. She is a large woman who looks not only terrified, but crazed. Her face is ashen. Her eyes are both dark and bloodshot. I do not know what she will do to me and am terrified. I am pushing the call button frantically.

Two nurses come in almost immediately and pull my curtains away from around my bed. I think perhaps they heard her scream too. The woman is still hovering over me, screaming. I feel like screaming too, but cannot, because of my injured vocal cord. One nurse is trying to calm me and is telling me the woman has just had brain surgery. She is the patient from the bed across the room from my bed.

Both nurses are now trying to restrain her and help her to her bed. Two more orderlies are running through the door. I'm happy that they have forgotten privacy and aren't replacing the curtain around my bed. I am so glad because I want to see what is happening, even though I am still scared! They appear to be scuffling with the woman. I hope they can subdue her without hurting her. I am less frightened now, and want to see what will happen next. One of the orderlies has leather restraints. I feel safer. The orderly is attaching the leather restraints to her wrists and ankles. (Leather restraints are like wide leather belts that can be attached to arms and ankles and anchored to a bed.) All four people are now carrying her to her bed. As they lay her on her bed and attach the restraints to the bed frame, I am so relieved that she cannot escape from her bed again. I realize she is totally confused and wonder what she is experiencing. I wish I could help. One of the nurses notices that I am watching and hastily pulls the curtain back around my bed.

It is now clear to me that I am really unsafe in this room. I feel extremely agitated from this experience and am shaking from the shock of it, feeling completely helpless again. The curtains around my bed make me feel more isolated and helpless. I know I cannot escape or protect myself from anyone who wants to hurt me. I cannot walk or run. I cannot protect myself in any way. I cannot even scream for help. My safety and my life are totally in the hands of others.

After this event, it seems that I cannot sleep at all. Every time I doze off, something happens to waken me again. I am attached to an IV and a blood pressure monitor that automatically takes my blood pressure every hour. The nurse also comes in to check me every hour and wakes me. I have to sleep sitting up because when I don't, I begin to choke.

Finally morning arrives; it is the day after the patient frightened me so. The medical team has decided that I am physically stable enough to move to a private room, further from the nurse's station.

I am now being wheeled into my new room on a stretcher. I wonder what it will be like. There is some sense of relief as I'm maneuvered through the door and learn that my private room has a window, so I can see outside, have some privacy, and experience a sense of distance from potentially violent patients.

CHAPTER 8
Privacy

The nurses are coming less frequently now, and although I like the privacy, I have the constant fear that I will choke to death when no one is here. I am now alone most of the time and no one is here to help me. I am experiencing fear in my chest; my throat feels tight. I am so relieved to see a nurse entering my room. She is carrying a tray with some cups on it as well as a container of ice cream. There is cold milk, water, hot cocoa, warm water and the ice cream. The nurse asks me to try all of them. I am fearful, but decide that if she will stay with me, I will experiment with drinking and eating. So, I try all of them. I discover that, after trial and error, I can swallow cold liquid. Warm liquid causes me to choke. I happily discover that I can swallow ice cream. A glimmer of hope arises within me. It is my first food since before my surgery!

Various members of my family have finally started to arrive and are beginning to take turns staying in the room with me during the day. My daughter Elaine is here now and I am feeling much safer and can relax a little.

The medical staff think I am doing well physically, but cannot understand my continued anxiety. They seem pleased with the fact that I have survived and do not appear to be brain damaged. However, every day they come in to evaluate me by asking "Do you know where you are?" Do you know what day it is today?" "What is your name?" and "Who is president of the United States?" I understand their need to evaluate me and the importance of monitoring me, but I am feeling slightly irritated by this and for about one minute toy with the idea of teasing them and pretending that I do not know my name. But I consciously let go of this mischievous thought, as I realize doing this could put me back in the four-bed ward, with the curtains. I believe I have somehow disappointed them because I am not feeling peaceful.

The senior neurology resident is striding into my room. It is the morning of the fifth day after my surgery. He is surrounded by a group of younger residents and interns. I'm listening as he presents my case to the group and am suddenly shocked as he dramatically rips the bandages off my head and neck. Smiling, he tells me, "Now you can get up and walk and then have a shower." I am still recovering from the sudden shock of having my bandages so abruptly although painlessly removed, but am also aware that I am hopeful after these positive words. He leaves now with his entourage and I soon discover that my hope will not last.

Almost immediately, after the residents and interns leave, two nursing assistants enter my room and tell me, "Now you can get up and walk to the bathroom." I am pleased that I am making fast progress and can graduate to walking. I stand, am able to walk three steps and now feel faint as I start to collapse and fall to the floor. The nursing assistants try to catch me as I am losing consciousness. They tell me that I was only out for a few moments and begin trying over and over to help me walk, However, every time I get into a standing position, within forty-five seconds, I become faint and have to sit down or I will faint. I know there is no way I can walk twelve feet to the bathroom. This problem continues during the days that follow. The doctors are notified about my predicament and many residents and interns come by to see for themselves what is happening to me.

Some doctors think that cutting the vagus nerve on one side of my body caused the problem. Others think it is poor circulation, and that I should wear a garment to constrict my blood vessels. Still others think my emotions are causing the problem. I try everything that is suggested and nothing works. I begin to wonder if I will ever be able to walk more than three feet again. One doctor prescribes that I must be taken out of my room in a wheelchair every day.

Leaving my room is somehow frightening! It feels unsafe, but I agree to go. The world outside my room seems harsh and too bright. I am still not able to watch TV and can only tolerate classical music. I do not want to leave the haven of this room! I can only whisper and I grieve for my powerful speaking voice. Sometimes I distract myself by remembering things that happened in the past that I believe shaped my life or are memorable. A memory that comes to my mind is a profound experience that long ago became an additional catalyst to my interest in the mind-body connection.

My Out-of-Body Experience

When I was eighteen years old, I was a freshman at the Ohio State University in the School of Nursing. It was after Christmas when I decided to go home to my mother's house for the weekend. The trip was uneventful and took only an hour. It seemed like a normal day. My mother and I decided to go shopping and enjoyed our companionship during our day together. It was Saturday night and I looked forward to going to bed early as the last few weeks at school had been hectic and stressful due to midterms and a new semester. Getting away for the weekend seemed like a mini-vacation.

After our pleasant day, I said an early good night to my mother and went to my room. I remember that it seemed so peaceful. I showered and climbed into my bed. Quickly, I drifted off to sleep.

I awoke with a start! I found myself floating in the air at the ceiling level of my room, and could see my inert body lying on my bed. I was filled with panic and wondered if I had died. I didn't like the predicament I was experiencing and didn't know what to do. I remember turning over and seeing details of the ceiling I had never noticed before. There was a spider web in one corner and a small crack in the dry wall. I wanted to be back in my body and didn't know how to get there. I remember that I decided to pray and silently asked God to let me live and be back in my body which was lying on the bed. Suddenly, I was back. My heart was racing. I was in a sweat and so grateful to be alive. After I gathered my composure, I decided not to tell anyone because I had never heard of such a thing. This experience made me believe in life after death. I had always wondered what death would be like. I thought perhaps now, I knew.

It is now three days since I was supposed to walk to the bathroom and still, no one can figure out why I faint every time I stand up for more than forty-five seconds. Every time I stand up my blood pressure plummets. Because no one seems to be able to solve this mystery, I have requested that an internist should be called in for a consultation. The physicians in the Neurosurgery Department do not usually consult with Internists, but agree to call one, when I insist with my weak voice.

The internist arrives two hours later. After reviewing my case, she decided that I should be given salt to raise my blood pressure, and the dosage of medicine to lower my blood pressure should be reduced. The surgeons agreed to try her recommendations.

I am now terrified that my blood pressure will once again go up to dangerous heights. This reminds me of the initial trauma of discovering my high blood pressure. However, I agree to try it. Two days later, I happily realize I am slightly improved. I can now walk four steps before fainting. However, my extreme anxiety and mistrust of the medical personnel is still baffling to me. If the tumor is gone, I wonder, why do I still experience anxiety? It must be from the Neurontin. I yearn again to be in touch with the feelings of oneness with God that I had during my vision right before my surgery.

Memories of Being Close to God

I felt closer to God than ever before when I experienced the vision, right before my surgery, of suddenly knowing without doubt, the reality that love, empathy and forgiveness are the only things that really matter. I knew then, and still know now, that this is the ultimate truth that lies at the heart of creation, and the only hope for the survival of mankind. I knew both in my head and in my heart then, that love can be found within all people. It is their connection to a loving source that enables empathy. Empathy is the ability to actually experience the feelings of others. Only then can we truly experience the full awareness of who we really are. Forgiveness is critical to the removal of negativity so each individual can fully and completely access their capacity for love and empathy. We must access this level of awareness in order to experience oneness with all people around the world, no matter what their spiritual path. This must happen in order to have world peace and solve the problems of our planet.

When human beings accept the fact that they are on the brink of death, most begin to question the meanings of their life. What was their mission, and have they completed it? Do they want to survive? Survival may depend upon having hope for a future. It is psychologically necessary to find meaning in life. This meaning could be for a loved one in their life or a cherished cause.

During my journey I experienced extreme helplessness. Even though I knew that my traumatic medical experiences were necessary to save my life, my helplessness magnified my suffering. The only way I could cope, was to use introspection and mindfulness to release myself from the prison of my helplessness and find refuge from the anxiety, pain, and desolation of the present.

I could escape into the past and allow myself to imagine a bright future. I remember thinking fleetingly, if I survive, I should write a book about this experience to help others. As my inner life became more intense, I also began to notice that I experienced the beauty of art and nature as never before. The meaning of my life, which I always knew at some level, but had not been previously focused upon, now became crystal clear. It was to help others. My career as a nurse and clinical psychologist had allowed me to fulfill that meaning. I also had the distinct awareness that I had more to do. These thoughts helped me survive my journey toward death and the subsequent changes in my voice.

I have now been in bed for several weeks without a shower and find myself dreaming of showers and imagine how good one would feel. I want so much to wash my hair. Then, one morning a miracle occurs. It turns out to be one of the most memorable, heartwarming events of my traumatic hospital experience. A muscular young male nurse arrives and makes a most wonderful offer. He says, "I brought my bathing suit to the hospital this morning, so that I can carry you to the shower and hold you while you wash your whole body, including your hair." I have some difficulty picturing the logistics of how this can actually work, but immediately agree! I never heard of such a thing, but it sounds wonderful to me. I realize now that I have lost my modesty. So many doctors, nurses, and various technicians have already invaded the privacy of my body by surgery, needles, poking and prodding, that it now seems silly to worry about such technicalities.

The nurse brings in several large towels and is asking me to wrap them around myself. Awkwardly, I am able to accomplish this. Now he effortlessly lifts me into his arms and carries me to the shower where warm water is already running. He carefully and artfully keeps my different body parts covered as I begin to wash them under the running water. (I wonder if he was trained to do this in nursing school.) Lastly, I am finally able to wash my hair. Now he turns off the shower and is wrapping me in dry towels, all the while, protecting my modesty by replacing one wet towel at a time with a dry towel. This process is difficult to describe, but it works. I know I will never forget this nurse. I feel so nurtured and cared for by a complete stranger whom I instinctively trust. And I never saw him again.

Another troubling symptom I experience is hearing music that is not there. It sounds like a dirge. I keep asking the nurses to turn it off. They tell me there is no music, but I don't believe them. My mindful self wonders if I am hallucinating. Now, my daughter Elaine informs me there is no music. I believe her, and am now able to ask the doctor about this "symptom." He explains that trauma to the acoustic nerve can cause this symptom and that it might or might not go away. I am relieved there is a physical reason for the music and believe that the nurses are relieved as well, now that I have stopped asking them to "turn it off." However, I am still continuing to hear it.

The surgeons have decided to discharge me after three weeks in the hospital. I can now consistently walk four feet and my blood pressure is stable.

Leaving the hospital is frightening. Even though I want to leave, I somehow feel safer in the hospital. Going home means that I will have to deal with the real world. I think about all the responsibilities as well as my compromised voice and wonder how I will be able to cope with this disability for the rest of my life. I realize I must stop thinking about the meaning of my life and what happened to me in the past. I must now face the future. I am now beginning to feel the effects of my unexpected handicap, the loss of my powerful speaking voice.

After my surgery I made arrangements to go to the same motel I had rented in the area for my family's and Brian's use during my entire stay at the hospital. I plan to use it now, while I am preparing to re-enter the real world.

My cousin Christina, who is a veterinarian from upstate New York, took a week from her busy schedule to travel to Stanford and be here to help me adjust! She has offered to take me to the motel and stay with me there until I go back to Santa Fe.

Daily, I am becoming more terrified of leaving the hospital. As the time for leaving draws near, I know I must face all the obstacles in my life and deal with whatever physical and emotional problems I have. I think about my home as well as all the bills I could not pay before I left. It all seems overwhelming. My plan is to spend this week in Palo Alto at the motel and continue to go back and forth to the hospital for further evaluation and help during this week to prepare me for the trip home.

Christina has arranged to borrow a wheelchair from the hospital and I am now putting on regular street clothes for the first time since the surgery. I need a lot of help to get dressed. It seems so strange to wear regular clothes and to be free of extraneous tubes on my body. I have begun to notice that my left arm has the sensation that it is going to "drop off." I cannot raise it higher than my shoulder. No one had prepared me for this problem.

Christina has packed up all my belongings and we are now being transported to the motel in a taxi. I am now able to proudly walk my four steps. It feels so wonderful to have my IV (intravenous feeding) removed. I no longer need it as I now can swallow bland liquids if they are cold. The intravenous line had been there for the entire three weeks! I am wondering how long I can live on ice cream and why I am still so anxious.

We will be in the large suite I rented for the family. It has two bedrooms, a bath, and a small kitchenette. Christina and I will be there alone until Brendalyn, my minister, comes at the end of the week.

Finally, we arrive at the motel. I am so glad to get here! I believe that I have made progress, but I have no clue as to how I can even begin to manage caring for myself.

Christina is wheeling me into my motel bedroom with the borrowed wheelchair and is now helping me into bed. We are discussing how to manage my food and figuring out how I can get to the bathroom. Christina suddenly has the brilliant idea of placing chairs four feet apart, in a trail to the bathroom and to the kitchen, so I can walk the four feet and then sit down for a minute or two before going to the next chair. I try it and, it works. I am able to manage the trips by myself. I'm beginning to experience my first small bit of independence, as well as have hope that all will someday be well.

It is now almost the end of the week in the motel and I am able to walk six feet before fainting. I am exhausted as is Christina, but my progress has continued. I have proudly noted my progress every day. I am less anxious but still a bit paranoid. My mindful self is helping me control these feelings to a large degree. I am still afraid to be alone and can easily choke. Eating is traumatic for me and I still feel that at any moment I can choke and die while eating.

The surgeons had to sever the nerve to my left vocal cord, leaving me with just one vocal cord. Human beings have two vocal cords which come together when a person swallows. I now only have the use of one vocal cord. I have been instructed to chew and swallow only on the side of my functional vocal cord. If I accidentally chew and swallow on the non-functional side, I might aspirate by breathing food into my lungs. Chewing and swallowing have become laborious as I struggle to eat. I discover that I cannot eat with other people present, as I have to concentrate on the eating process so intently. I fear any distraction could prove fatal to me. I am constantly afraid of aspiration. I cannot speak during a meal or pay attention to any conversation, or I start to choke. I have to eat differently from ever before, since I can only swallow on the right side. Now, I can only manage to swallow liquids like ice cream or smoothies.

During this week while we are staying at the motel, I have been asked by my medical team to return to Stanford Medical Center for two tests to evaluate the results of my surgery. They include hearing tests and another MRI. I am aware that I still maintain my mistrust of most of the medical personnel and depend on Christina for emotional support during the tests. It is like going into battle again, while suffering from extreme battle fatigue.

My psychologist-self reassures me by reminding me that I am probably suffering from Post Traumatic Stress Disorder (PTSD). I keep telling myself my battle is over, not knowing other battles are yet to be faced.

CHAPTER 9
The Long Journey Home

While Christina and I are at this motel, I decide to become proactive and, in addition to all my appointments at Stanford, have called alternative health care experts from various venues to come and work with me. I feel so relieved to now have alternative medical help. An acupuncturist, a Feldenkrais practitioner, and a counselor have been coming here to help me.

The high point of the week is a real bath in the motel bathtub. Christina has drawn the water and is standing by in case I need her. I am unsure if I can coordinate my body well enough to get in and out of the tub. I finally lift my leg over the side of the tub and successfully lower myself into the warm bath water. It is wonderful! I am looking forward to going to a beauty parlor tomorrow to get my hair washed and styled. I hope I can do it.

It is the next day. Christina wheels me into the beauty salon. She and I explain my physical problems to the beauty parlor operator. She seems to understand and is willing to help. Now I am tentatively laying my head back in the shampoo bowl as I always did in the past. However, this is different!

I am feeling dizzy and begin to panic. I'm beginning to choke from putting my head back. Christina is holding my hand and helping the esthetician support my head and neck so I can sit up at various intervals as she washes my hair. My neck is so weak, which I didn't realize before. This process of having a shampoo is terrifying, but I am determined to pursue it. I believe I will feel so much better after my hair is washed and I can transform into a more normal looking person. I so want to look normal when I get back to Santa Fe and see all my friends.

The end of the week has arrived so quickly. Christina must return to her veterinary practice in New York, and my children have already returned to their jobs, after spending time with me in the hospital. The minister of the Unity Church of Santa Fe, almost unbelievably, offered to fly to Stanford and assist me in my travels home to Santa Fe. Reverend Brendalyn Batchelor is the person who orchestrated all the prayers and volunteers who helped me. I gratefully accepted her offer and my heart was moved by her gestures. The plan is for her to spend two days at the motel, in our suite here, and then help me on the trip home. I am now beginning to really think of the future!

It is my last day in this motel. Brendalyn and Christina are now helping me prepare to go home to Santa Fe. We will need a wheel chair to get me through the airport and Brendalyn is arranging for one to be available. I feel like such a burden and only hope that someday I will be able to walk and eat and talk normally. I wonder how I can ever pay back others for what they are doing for me. I am somewhat embarrassed at the thought of being wheeled through the airport. Brendalyn told me she has organized people from the church to help me for my first month at home. The church board president, Carolyn Doherty, even volunteered to cook all my food for a month. Others offered to take me to appointments, and still others to help in various other ways. Brendalyn even arranged for an accountant from church to help straighten out my bills and business affairs.

I know I need all the help I can get. I am not yet ready to live on my own alone! My situation of such extreme helplessness is painful for me. I feel so needy and dependent on so many others for survival. I have no choice but to accept all the help, but am for some reason, experiencing guilt and shame about doing so. I even find myself searching for ways to blame myself, even though I know I have not caused my present dilemma. I am so thankful for everyone's help. This is all so overwhelming to me, that I feel tears rolling down my face.

Finally, the day has come to leave Palo Alto. I am much improved and am now able to walk ten steps to a taxi cab. Christina will get a flight later in the day back to New York.

Christina is hugging me goodbye and waives me off, as I get into the cab with Brendalyn. Christina and I both have tears in our eyes. Mine are tears of gratitude for my life and her help. I suspect hers are the same.

Going through the airport and being wheeled in a wheelchair in the world outside the hospital is a new experience for me. I look at all the people walking quickly around the airport to their various destinations and I feel so wistful. I am wondering if I will ever be able to rush about that way and function normally again. No one is sure, but I am determined. It is an interesting new experience to be allowed to pre-board the plane home. I will be wheeled down the ramp by Brendalyn.

This is embarrassing! I know I am a burden to everyone, but at the same time, I am so thankful for Brendalyn's help and consideration. I wonder if I will ever be able to help others again. Who will I become? How will I be able to pay everyone back for all they are doing for me?

My voice seems worse. It has become a weaker whisper since I got out of the hospital. I am beginning to focus on all the things I will face at home. Coping with the unpaid bills, my house, my kitten Maurice, and all the details of survival seems overwhelming. I am glad to be going home, but am dreading facing the situations I know I will encounter. I also have clients who are waiting for me to recover so they can resume therapy, although I am not sure if I will ever be able to do therapy with patients again. As I look out the window of the plane, I am beginning to think about the many crises I have survived in the past several months.

Crises

After surviving my journey toward death, I viewed the world differently. I now needed to make sense of my new world.

I remembered that several years earlier, I had consulted with two support groups of both men and women who had experienced open heart surgery. Everyone in both groups reported that they were keenly aware of the fact they had been very close to death. Everyone there freely described how they had felt traumatized by their surgeries. There was a higher than normal divorce rate among the group members. Both men and women had changed their lives in major ways. Many had changed their religious and spiritual beliefs, and still others felt they now were more aware of what was really important in their lives as well as in the world. Many changed their occupations. All reported experiencing high levels of crisis, and some members were dealing with an Existential Crisis.

Existential Crisis

An existential crisis is a deep questioning and unsettled state about one's very being, sense of self, and personal meaning in the world. One's relationship to everyone and everything around them is brought into question. It can cause extreme psychological pain for the individual experiencing it. He or she may feel lost. These feelings can permeate all aspects of a person's life. Aging, extensive exposure to death, and various kinds of losses can create this experience. Patients experiencing unexpected traumatic medical catastrophes and later unexpected handicaps are in crisis and may experience extreme existential confusion. They may wonder if they have fulfilled their mission in life and actualized their full potential. Their crisis may become a further catalyst to a continued search for the meaning of their lives. Acceptance of where you are in the here and now is a first step toward resolution. I did not experience an existential crisis from my medical trauma and unexpected handicap, but the crisis related to my trauma was of very high intensity.

However, I did experience an existential crisis from my work as a psychologist, years before this journey. It was related to my work with several patients who reported ritual satanic cult abuse. The information I heard was almost beyond my comprehension. My view of a world that could include such evil, changed forever. It was no longer as safe as I previously thought. I observed colleagues who were also experiencing crises related to this type of information. It took me about three years to reconfigure my life and discover who I was in my changed world.

A crisis of any kind offers both opportunity and danger. There are different intensities of crises. For the sake of discussion, I will categorize them as low intensity, medium intensity, and high intensity. Examples of low-intensity crises are: a leak in the hot-water heater causes damages to your wood floors; the breakdown of your oven as you are preparing Thanksgiving dinner for ten people; or the loss of your billfold with all your credit cards in it. Medium-intensity crises could include: loss of a job; a breakup with a significant other; or a small fire in your garage. Examples of crises usually accepted as high-intensity could include: divorce; death of a spouse or child; being faced with one's own death; or a major illness.

Since every individual perceives their own reality dependent upon who they are and their past experiences, they also perceive critical events differently. What would be high intensity crisis for one person, might not be for another person.

The following is an example of different perceptual experiences of a critical event by different individuals. Consider two married couples. Husband and wife in couple A, have been happily married for twenty years and are lovers as well as friends. They have been faithful to each other. Husband and wife in couple B, have also been married for twenty years, but harbor deep animosity for each other and have only stayed together for the sake of their children. Both partners in couple B have had extramarital love affairs and wish they could be with different partners. Suddenly, both couples lose a spouse due to an auto accident. The intensity of the crisis for the same event would obviously be different for each survivor.

As mentioned earlier, crises can offer both danger and opportunity. There is meaning as well as danger and opportunity present in every crisis. Consider the leaky hot water heater. The hot water heater needs to be replaced as well as the floors refinished. The family learns how to protect the house so, if the new hot water heater fails, the floors will not be harmed. Happiness and feelings of security are restored. Crises of all intensities can be motivating and energizing as well as painful. They facilitate changing whatever needs to be changed in order restore normality to life.

High-intensity crises, such as being near death can generate soul searching as well as deep suffering. Major crises sometimes take years to resolve to the point where one can reconfigure one's life around the traumatic events of the crisis.

The plane is touching down. We are in Albuquerque. I am both elated and scared. I am aware of how we are reversing the process I went through when Brian and I flew to Palo Alto for my surgery. I walk the few steps needed to get into a wheelchair outside of the airplane. Now Brendalyn is wheeling me through the concourse and proceeding to the luggage area. She is claiming our baggage and wheeling me outside. I can smell the New Mexico air. It is so pure! I'll wait here in this wheelchair while she brings her van around to get me and take us to Santa Fe.

Finally, the van is here! I can stand up and walk the few steps to it. Brendalyn helps me into it. We are now beginning the hour-long drive from the Albuquerque airport to Santa Fe. It is familiar and feels safe.

It is an hour since we left the airport and Brendalyn is finally pulling her van into my driveway. There is no wheelchair, but there are three people who are rushing out to greet us. They include two church members and Brian. I know I must walk through my garage, down a flight of steps and then about 30 feet to my bedroom, but I don't know if I can do it!

I don't remember the details of how I made it to my bedroom. I believe I walked part way, and was carried part of the way. I am so amazed and grateful for all the people helping me. Since I no longer have a wheelchair, I wonder how I can manage everything. Should I buy a wheelchair? Will I ever be able to lead a normal life again?

I am finally home, but am so exhausted, I do not have the strength or energy to unpack my suitcase or fix food for myself. I am in bed. All I can do is lie in bed. Even though I feel useless, helpless and anxious, there is something very calming about being home. I think how thankful I am that I did not have cancer.

My kitten, Maurice, is such a delight! He wants to cuddle with me and is purring constantly as he snuggles against me in bed. This is greatly comforting.

There is a forest fire fifty miles away from Santa Fe at this time, the first one I have ever experienced in New Mexico. I have the irrational fear that the fire will reach me and I will be helpless to escape, since I can only walk nine or ten feet and do not know if I can even drive my car. Being dependent on others for my life is almost beyond my comprehension. It is a startlingly new experience. Being dependent in the hospital was one thing, but experiencing it in my own home is somehow even more frightening. I ask Brian if he will promise to take me out of Santa Fe if the fire gets too close. He reassures me that he will. My mindful self tells me that my level of panic is not appropriate. Why is my anxiety still here? I still have some fear of dying, but now most of my fears are about the future.

True to her word, the church member, Carolyn, is here and has already supplied my kitchen with food. She says she is prepared to cook and shop for me for a month. Others are on a team that will be available to drive me to appointments whenever necessary. Still others have offered to stay with me for periods during the day and one church member, who is an accountant, is already working on piles of unread messages and bills that I hastily left on my dining room table. Brian says he will come every day for two weeks and help in any way he can when he is available. Everything seems under control. I now only need one chair between me and the bathroom where my shower already has a seat in it. The simple things I always took for granted now become the focus of my attention. I am now spending a lot of time in the here-and-now.

CHAPTER 10

The Decision

I am lying in my bed, pondering my situation. It is my first morning at home. I am assessing the damages to my mind and body after what feels like my almost miraculous survival. I can now, very seriously, begin to plan for the future.

Before returning home, I made the decision to do everything I could, to return to a normal life and learn how to live with, and improve, my weak voice. The following is a synopsis of my experiences.

My anxiety was gone a month after my return home. It had most probably been caused by the withdrawal effects of the drug Neurotin. My emotions quickly returned to normal. I treated my physical problems with exercise, biofeedback to lower my blood pressure, if needed, prayer, meditation, energy healing, homeopathy, and Feldenkrais, to name a few. I was so happy to read books again and regained full use of my mind. I was able to drive my car and began to lead a normal life. Within six weeks, I could walk a mile or more.

Speech therapy of various kinds was helpful. I learned to swallow and eat regular food. Two months after arriving home, I was able to deliver a short talk about dissociative disorders to a group of psychologists. (I used a microphone.) I developed and wrote about a model to demonstrate how unexpected handicaps are different from other handicaps.

Three months after my surgery, I traveled to Italy and spent two weeks there. Two years after my surgery, I decided I wanted to fulfill a life-long dream of becoming an artist. Since my surgery, I had begun to experience the beauty of art and nature as never before.

Brian and I drifted apart soon after I was fully recovered. We both realized we were not destined to be a long-term couple.

I enrolled in the Santa Fe Community College's art program and, after several years of classes, graduated with an Associate's Degree in Fine Arts. I was startled by some of my paintings, especially when I realized they were expressing some of the suffering I had experienced during my journey. I had not realized how therapeutic the classes were for me until I painted those pictures.

Two-and-a-half months after my surgery, I began to see patients again. I was happy to discover that my soft voice did not inhibit my effectiveness as a psychologist in clinical practice.

My friends rallied around me as I continued to dismiss the trauma from my mind and life. Three years after my surgery, I remarried. Richard, my husband, is a research psychologist who has dedicated his life to helping learning disabled children. All was well in my life.

At times, I still think about the many things I learned during my journey toward death. One of these was directly related to my father.

When I find myself thinking of my father, I remember how much he cared for his patients. Even though I was a child, he often shared with me his worries and cares about seriously ill patients. When one of his patients died, I remember how my father grieved. I saw tears in his eyes. His caring and love for his patients seem somehow related to the revelations I experienced right before my surgery. The love and compassion that surrounded me then was so pure and has now become an absolute part of my life. I wish I could feel it at all times, but can only feel it once in a while. It is easy to access when I meditate. I wonder if my father may have felt those emotions as he cared for his patients. Sometimes I yearn for that all knowing feeling of oneness with all.

As I continue to think about my father, I have become keenly aware of the emotional pain and disillusionment of many of the doctors of today, who have neither time nor energy to care about their patients in the same way he did. I am saddened by the knowledge that the practice of medicine has become deprofessionalized. (A profession is an occupation that has its own code of ethics and is controlled by a professional group that has the power to sanction or reward its members for their work.) Groups such as the American Medical Association, The American Psychiatric Association, and the American Psychological Association, still exist, but for the most part lack the power to monitor how practices are run.

The practice of medicine was previously a calling, similar to that of the calling to become a priest. Now, insurance companies control most medical practices and determine to a large extent how physicians treat their patients as well as how much time should be spent with each patient. I have been told the average time spent is fifteen minutes. I have spoken with several physicians who were clients of mine who have become so disheartened with how they must run their medical practices that they have left the practice of medicine. (When physicians are unable to give the type of care or treatment they believe is best for their patients, they inevitably become frustrated.)

Fifty years ago, physicians had the time to care for their patients in interactions that were meaningful, and heartfelt. True loving compassion was present. Both doctor and patient knew each other well. There was an authentic bond between them. This was rewarding to both the patient and their physician. My father taught me that loving compassion in itself is healing to others. As I ponder our country's health care dilemmas, I realize I am presently helpless to change these conflicts and can only hope social change can somehow return professionalism and true caring to medical practice.

As I return to the here-and-now during the writing of this book, my thoughts of my father validate my belief that loving compassion in all helping professions positively affects outcomes.

I can report that Richard and I have now been happily married for thirteen years. We share our adult children and grandchildren. I no longer think of myself as a victim of trauma. We live in Santa Fe, and I continue to work with clients. Richard and I attend Unity Church together.

Now something unexpected and frightening is occurring again. This morning, as I opened my eyes, I became aware that I have not been feeling well for several days. It has now been sixteen years since my medical traumas. While writing this book about my struggles for survival, and the meanings related to them, memories of the past seem to have triggered the return of many negative feelings that I experienced sixteen years ago. I also realize that I am continuing to try to better understand my past experiences by writing about them. This awareness is related to a totally unexpected and surprising experience that occurred last night!

An Epiphany in the Dark of Night

As I went to sleep, I was thinking of my past medical traumas and attempting to discover even deeper meanings of them. I am accustomed to ideas coming into my mind after I go to sleep, so I usually have a pen and pencil available if I wake up during the night so I can scribble any insights I have generated that come to me during the night while sleeping. I found from experience that, if I don't write them down, I usually forget them by morning and cannot retrieve them.

On this particular night, I abruptly awoke around 2:00 a.m. I was so startled by the new and unusual thoughts racing through my mind, that I abruptly sat straight up in bed. It felt as though my mind was being filled with information, almost faster than I could think. It felt like a deluge. I knew I must write it down. It was almost as though I was commanded to write it down. I felt a low level of panic when my paper and pencil were nowhere to be found! I knew it was imperative that I get up and find them quickly, before the deluge of information ceased. I knew without doubt, that this was important!

I rushed into my home office and snatched the first thing I could find to write on. It was several pieces of computer paper and I quickly found a ball-point pen. The information I received took several hours to write down. All I could do was write as fast as I was able. Then, the deluge finally slowed and stopped. I felt complete and drained, but excited as I returned to my bed. I fell into a deep sleep almost immediately. When I woke in the morning, I remembered the episode, but true to form, could not remember what I had written. I hurried to my office to see what I had written. The content was amazing and complete! I will share it with you in the next chapter.

I now again have a headache, and for some reason once again have to take my blood pressure. (I have not found it necessary to do this for a very long time.) I place the cuff on my arm and press the button. The monitor registers 180/110!

It has now been sixteen years since my journey to the door of death. I have fully returned to life in the world, as I knew it outside the hospital. My clinical practice has grown and I freely give talks about various psychological topics when invited. I no longer worry about my new voice. It is lower and husky and I need a microphone for my talks. These changes are part of who I am now. I continue to be happily married and have been busy balancing my practice with writing books. When I have time, I also enjoy my pursuit of art.

Since I was not feeling well recently and my blood pressure was elevated, I became alarmed enough to think I should go to the local emergency room to discover what was causing it. I asked Richard to drive me. I was frightened again for the first time in many years, as I had begun to wonder if I was having a recurrence of another pheochromocytoma, in some other part of my body. This felt like a flashback! It was during this worrisome time that I received the unexpected information in the middle of the night. I believe receiving the information was the result of being stimulated again to make further sense out of my long-past trauma.

Richard was a calming influence and reassured me as he drove to the hospital. We were both somewhat anxious and concerned as to why my blood pressure was so high. I even began to experience the old, but familiar, terror beginning to rise in the pit of my stomach and reverberate in my throat. I was again immediately admitted to the inner sanctum of the emergency room. This felt like déjà vu!

The emergency-room doctor said, "We must explore the possibility that you have another pheochromocytoma." The nurse quickly started an IV and administered a strong drug to bring down my blood pressure. I wondered if it would work this time, or would it be like sixteen years ago when my blood pressure would not go down? My blood pressure quickly returned to normal. I felt relief washing over me, and was so relieved that I remember feeling a bit giddy, but still deeply concerned. I wondered what could be causing my elevated blood pressure.

After numerous medical tests, and even a later trip to the Mayo clinic, I discovered that I did not have another pheochromocytoma. Everything seemed normal. I then decided that my problem must be emotional. I knew that I needed to explore all the possibilities of things that could have created these psychological reactions. A profound realization finally dawned on me! I had been so immersed in writing this book, that I had been unaware of the actual physiological effects upon my body from reliving my sixteen year old traumatic experiences every day, as I wrote.

In addition, I also remembered that my husband and I had been watching "Grey's Anatomy" on Netflix almost every evening for several weeks while I was writing. (For those readers who are not familiar with the show, it is a highly dramatic series, about emergency room doctors and residents dealing with extremely traumatic cases similar to mine. The dramas are extremely realistic and at some points, bloody.) I realized this series had also been reminding me of some of my past traumatic medical emergencies.

Since I had an elevated blood pressure that needed strong medication again, I decided to stop watching that TV show. I was so glad that the parts of this book that were the most traumatic for me to write, had already been written!

I decided to prescribe a two-week vacation from writing for myself. After the vacation my blood pressure magically returned to normal, with no medication. I realized that I now still felt like avoiding anything that could remind me of my journey to the door of death. This avoidance is, as readers may surmise, a symptom of PTSD. I realized that I had re-traumatized myself through writings about my trauma and from viewing "Grey's Anatomy!"

Before writing this book, I had placed the traumatic events related to my medical emergencies out of my mind and seldom thought about them. They had become a part of my life history and seemed to no longer have an emotional impact on me. Now, this had temporarily changed.

As I continued to mindfully observe myself, I realized that I was feeling a sense of embarrassment about my psychological reactions, and wondered if I should keep this experience to myself or incorporate it into this book. As I pondered my embarrassment, I knew that I must not only share these reactions, but also share what came to me in the night.

The information I knew I must share with you briefly before describing my epiphany, was to identify the meaning of my avoidance behavior, to discuss suffering and PTSD, to assess what can be done to improve the situation in health care settings, and the treatment of spiritual issues related to traumatic medical experiences.

Almost immediately, the significant meaning of my avoidance behavior became clear! My reactions were a perfect example of how the mind can affect the body. (This will be pursued in my next book which deals with issues related to an insider's experiences with alternative methods of healing.)

Many people, even though physically healed, are so affected emotionally, that they are unable to return to productive lives. It is imperative that both health care professionals, as well as families and friends of patients experiencing crisis become aware of these emotional issues.

What Can Be Done in Health Care Settings

It is clear from my experiences, the considered research, and anecdotal reports mentioned earlier, that severe emotional trauma and suffering can occur at high enough levels to cause PTSD in patients receiving diagnostic tests and treatment. Some patients whose physical bodies and emotional stability have been affected by both physical trauma and drugs qualify for the diagnosis of PTSD.

This knowledge will help more patients adjust, receive appropriate treatment and better survive to lead normal and fruitful lives. The identification and utilization of methods to enhance resilience in these patients is also important to increased survival rates. Resilience can be taught by therapists, nurses, and other health care personnel who have been trained in these methods. Friends and families of traumatized patients can better support their loved ones, if they understand that many of the abnormal emotional states their loved ones exhibit are normal, and most likely temporary. Former and current patients may draw comfort from knowing that others have been through similar crises and survived. They will feel understood and less alone in their suffering.

A major key to patient survival is to find meaning in their trauma. Meanings are individual for each person.

They could be spiritual changes within themselves, a desire to help others, related to a relationship with a loved one or, something entirely different that is specific to that person. The meaning may be temporarily hidden. I believe two meanings for me were the heightened awareness I developed as a result of the trauma and the discovery of my ability to write about my learnings in order to help others.

There are nurses, psychologists, social workers, and counselors who have specialized in working with trauma. Many of today's training programs now teach how to counsel their clients with spiritual issues, as well as how to help them develop resilience and mindfulness. Meditation is extremely helpful and can also be easily and quickly taught to patients if they are able to concentrate.

Treatments for PTSD have evolved in the past few years. They have gone far beyond psychotherapy and now include various energy medicine techniques, as well as the use of neuro-programming. I will not describe them here, as they are extensive.

There is now greater awareness of these issues within the medical establishment than there was in the past, but there is still more to accomplish in critical care settings.

Emotional recovery is also enhanced by experiencing a support system. A support system is comprised of people around you who care for your well-being. It could include family, friends, medical personnel, counselors, spiritual communities, or other groups to which you belong. Various therapies both traditional and non-traditional can facilitate both emotional and physical healing. Health care systems could and should provide this needed help.

The information I received in the middle of the night is relevant to all the experiences, traumas, and suffering I have experienced during my lifetime, and provides a key toward understanding one's self and others. Here it comes.

CHAPTER 11
The Epiphany

The information that seemed placed in my mind in the middle of the night resulted in a model of human behavior that can help explain how and why individuals around the world perceive the world and one another so differently. It also demonstrates how a major crisis can shatter perceptions and thus create the need for an individual to create a new and different perceptual organization, in order to feel safe in the world. This model labels each person's perceptual organization as a myth because even for the most enlightened among us, true reality is still beyond the reach of our human consciousness. One's perceptions may or may not have anything to do with reality. Everyone must have a myth or dream in order to feel safe in their world. Myths are composed of rules and roles that they believe will help them meet their needs and obtain their goals. So my model is called the Model of Progressive Myths.

It is generally accepted that there is a lack of agreement among scientists, religious scholars, philosophers, political parties, and others about the nature of reality. Individuals, as well as all social systems are motivated to develop their own myths in order to make sense of their perceived realities. Since individuals are not the only ones who have and build myths, it is important to understand that every social grouping to which we belong also has its own mythical system in order to function in the world. Examples of these systems include scientific groups, various occupational groups, religious groups, spiritual groups, philosophical groups, political parties, geographic groups, and others.

My major focus here will be on individual myth building. The sudden loss of one's individual myth can cause temporary or long term confusion, emotional pain, and anxiety. In the extreme, it can create an existential crisis as described earlier. However, the destruction of one's myth may also result in positive outcomes such as heightened levels of consciousness, better understanding of others, a happier life with greater meaning, and freedom to view the world in new ways. Loss of one's myth can also free an individual or group to reconfigure their thinking and enable them to build a new and more functional myth.

The new myth is based on new learnings about one's self, others, and the world. The individual or group building a new myth can then be described as progressive myth builders.

This model is applicable to everyone and every group to which we belong. It can aid us in our struggles to exist and prosper in our very complicated world. This is a world where we all struggle to survive, care for our loved ones, and know what is right. The Progressive Myth Model has the potential to stimulate empathy and enhance tolerance and understanding of others.

Myths do not precipitously shatter unless a major crisis occurs. Original myths can remain in place for a person's entire lifetime.

After receiving this model in the middle of the night, I, at first, thought I might have read it somewhere in the past, but could not remember where. I spent the next several weeks searching to discover its origin. I was not able to find anything like it. As I searched, I realized this model also made sense of my own life.

Next, I shared it with friends and family. The model also helped explain their lives and major travails. Several people close to me found it personally helpful. I decided to consult with several other psychologists about the model. They said they were impressed with it and encouraged me to continue developing it. My next step was to introduce it to patients and determine if it was helpful to them. I began by sharing it with five patients. Every one reported that it was helpful to them. Two patients believed they had been freed to give up some constricted ways of thinking that they had been using to guide themselves as they experienced their world. It became clear to me that this model was congruent with other forms of therapeutic interventions. So here is a synopsis of the different types of myths and their effects upon individuals and groups.

Progressive Life Myths

The name of the model I received in the night is Progressive Life Myths. We all live within the particular myths we have created, which represent our dreams and interpretation of our world. (A myth is a story serving to explain something. It may be a fictitious story.)

Personal myths come into existence early in life to create a method to feel safe in the world. One's first myth is usually taught by our parents, family members, family friends, neighbors, television, and the internet. Personal learnings result in the development of rules to live by to guide us through life. Some of those rules are never actually stated, only implied. Early experiences, as well as heredity, influence the first myth we create.

Myths involve not only rules to live by, but roles as well. Roles are how we identify ourselves within our own individual myth as well as within the myths of the social groups to which we belong. These are varied: Some examples of roles we are given, or decide to take on are limitless, and could include: victim, caregiver, rescuer, hero, winner, loser, lover, provider, problem child, warrior, identified patient, mother, father, criminal. The list is long.

Our myths can help us lead fruitful and rewarding lives, or potentially have the danger of entrapping us in dysfunctional behavior. Problems can occur if the myth is so absolute that it is not open to receiving and using new information. If this occurs, both individuals and social groups become inhibited in their ability to absorb new knowledge and raise consciousness.

Some children, after a time, reject their parents' efforts to help them build their own myths. One reason for this rejection is that some children may be in the normal struggle to differentiate from parental control. Another reason is that still others may be exposed to information outside their family teachings that cause them to reject their parent's myth system. Some children's opposing myths are dysfunctional and can result in a crisis fairly quickly and others may last a lifetime and become either extremely functional or extremely dysfunctional.

Not only do all individuals experience their personal myths, but myth-building is necessary for all human social systems. Myth-building expands far beyond the individual and includes couples, families, neighborhoods, cities, states, countries, hemispheres, all human beings in the world.

Every work group has its own myth. Professional groups such as lawyers, doctors, scientists, traditional physicists, quantum physicists, clergy, philosophers, and psychologists, have their own myths. All human beings and the groups to which they belong are attempting to define reality.

Types of Myths

Impermeable-Absolute and Permeable-Expansive Myths

Some myths are experienced as absolutely true. Individuals within an impermeable myth are unable to expand within their myth as the world changes and new information emerges. Impermeable boundaries around a myth prevent new information from entering.

This was exemplified by the historical behavior of many people, when it was discovered that the world is round. People with impermeable myths were unable to incorporate that information into their myth. Many held on to their flat-world beliefs to their dying day. An example of a modern-day belief that is found in an impermeable myth for some people today, is the belief that climate change does not exist.

Individuals who have permeable-expansive myths allow new information into their myths, at least for consideration. This allows their myth to be modified, and they are able to also comfortably share information with others. It is possible for an expansive myth to be held for an entire lifetime, modifying it to meet the individual's needs in a changing world.

Trapped within an Absolute Myth

Psychological problems can occur for those who become trapped within an absolute myth as they are unable to incorporate new information, use it, and learn from mistakes.

I remember a client named Stephanie who was miserable and unhappy for many reasons. She had recently realized that her adult children had been taking advantage of her by constantly asking for money and favors. They treated her badly and accused her of not being a good mother. When money was not forthcoming, her children would have nothing to do with her and disappeared from her life.

Stephanie did not feel loved by anyone. She believed her mother and sisters hated her and perceived that everyone in the world had treated her badly. She identified herself as a victim and her husband as her major victimizer. He had been an alcoholic who had died in an auto accident ten years earlier. Now she was alone and had to care for herself.

Stephanie believed that she had been handicapped in her endeavors in life by her entire family. It seemed to her that no matter where she went or what she did, she was a failure, and it was all her husband's fault.

When I first met Stephanie, she was in a major crisis. Her myth was falling apart. She was a very angry person. Her world made no sense to her. I perceived kindness in her eyes, despite her anger. I knew that she was indeed suffering.

After several weeks of therapy, it became clear that Stephanie believed she was entitled to a good life, as she had always been a "good girl." When life became difficult, she could not cope. This was due to her Absolute Mythical Belief system. She was unable to absorb new information and learn different ways to deal with her life. She had become trapped within a mythical belief system that prevented her from learning better ways to handle life after her husband died. All she could do was blame others for any problems she experienced.

The rules of her myth were; "If I am a good girl and do what I am told, I will get everything I want and live happily ever after. I am entitled to be taken care of forever." The role she chose in her myth was that of a victim.

I soon discovered that Stephanie had never learned to empathize with others. She could deal with problems only by becoming angry and distraught, while blaming others for all her difficulties. She had been unable to reconfigure her life after the loss of her husband and remained angry with him for dying and leaving her alone to deal with life, ten years after his death. Stephanie felt entitled to his continued care for the rest of her life.

After taking her history, I wondered: How could this have happened to her? What therapeutic help could be used to help her? I realized that her parents had taught her the rules of her myth, that by being a "good girl" and looking pretty everything she desired would be given to her. "If you are a good girl and look pretty, you will have a perfect life." This parental approach led her to create the mythic dream of a perfect life with no problems, by being beautiful and doing the "right thing."

Stephanie was finally ready to break out of her myth. The crisis with her children had helped her. When I explained the concept of progressive myths to her, she almost immediately decided this concept made some sense of all her problems. She was able to gradually stop blaming herself and others for all her problems and was ready to discover and learn new ways of handling traumatic life situations. Stephanie learned to empathize with some of her family members who had been upset with her. Her progress was rapid. Stephanie had been trapped in an absolute-impermeable myth.

My First Myth

My first myth had a dream scenario. It was a permeable-expansive myth. I was not trapped. The scenario was that my parents would always love me and I would be safe forever. I believed that I would always be taken care of and that my parents would live into old age. Others would always respect me and I wouldn't miss my parents too much when they died, since by then, I would be grown up, married, and have children of my own. My children would take care of me, if I ever needed help.

The rules I accepted were that I must do well in school, I must be honest and kind, I must be a high achiever, I must smile a lot and never cry, and I must always do what I was told by my parents and teachers. My role was to be a "good girl."

I believed that if I kept all the rules, my dreams would come true. Prince Charming would arrive some day and sweep me away to live happily ever after. I would never want for anything.

This myth was shattered by my father's death when I was thirteen years old. After his death, I had to be strong, and provide emotional support for my mother. My role was changed to becoming the emotional caregiver for my mother.

I had experienced a moderate intensity crisis and was no longer clear about who I was, and what I needed to do to feel safe in the world. As I entered high school, I perceived there was a prejudice against fatherless teenagers. I had lost the social standing I had previously experienced as the daughter of a prominent physician. I had three half-sisters whom I loved and had believed loved me. Now, after my father died, they wanted nothing to do with me or my mother.

My mother now had to work to support us and did not have much time to nurture me. I felt like an outsider as I could not relate to the "giggly girls" my age. I knew about death and loneliness. They did not. High school was an emotional struggle, even though I had several friends who were also outsiders. I no longer studied hard nor worked up to my potential, but still did above average work. Being a "good girl" was no longer enough. Since this crisis had catapulted me out of my myth, I was forced to create a new myth, with new rules and roles.

This meant I must open my mind to create a new reality. This can be a daunting and terrifying task for anyone, depending on the perceived intensity of the crisis. But the destruction of every myth also has a benefit. I learned I could be strong and independent. I realized I could survive, even if I didn't fit in. I now believe that even though I felt abandoned by my father and stepsisters, I knew I could survive. In this time between myths, I was in the process of creating a new myth.

Functional and Dysfunctional Myths

When children create a functional myth, the feelings of security it provides enables them to grow and survive in a pleasant and positive way. They can experience feelings of peace and safety. Life seems predictable. These children are happy and life makes sense to them. They function well in the world.

When children create a dysfunctional myth, life can become anxiety-producing and frightening. This type of myth can result in antisocial behavior. Life may become chaotic for both parents and children. The child's actions run counter to societal norms.

A Dysfunctional Myth

I remember a boy, I will call Andrew, whose family inadvertently helped him create a dysfunctional myth for himself. Unfortunately, Andrew was born into a chaotic family. His parents were well intentioned, law abiding, and kind people who said they attended church regularly.

Andrew was thirteen years old when I met him. He had become seriously unmanageable. Andrew had been caught shop lifting on two occasions, refused to complete his work at school, and was rude to the teacher. He bullied other children, and refused to dress like the other boys in his class. His hygiene was terrible and other students complained to the teachers about his strong body odor. He looked disheveled and his clothes were in disarray. On day he dyed his hair green before going to school

The week before I met him, he had stolen his mother's car keys and driven her car into a tree. He was in trouble with the law. On several occasions Andrew started fights at school and other children had been severely injured. The school decided that he should be placed in classes for the emotionally disturbed.

Andrew's parents were very upset when they learned of the recommendation and decided to remove him from school to avoid the placement. They did not want him to be "labeled" as emotionally disturbed and decided to hire a lawyer to help him evade his problems with the police as well as tutors to teach him at home.

After he was taken out of school, he would not cooperate with his parents at all and spent most of his time on the internet. His academic achievement was two years behind grade level. His tutors tried to help him, but his academic progress was minimal.

Andrew's parents then asked for help for the first time. They were both medical doctors who were very responsible within their work settings. They abided by the myths and roles of the medical profession.

When I met them they proudly stated that they had provided Andrew with everything he wanted. They could not understand what could be the cause of his bad behavior. Their belief had been, that if he was loved and kept happy, he would naturally develop into a loving, caring person.

But Andrew's home was chaotic as both parents worked irregular schedules and often decided on the spur of the moment to go out late at night. Since it was too late to get a babysitter, they always took Andrew with them. From the time he was an infant, he was often awakened in the middle of the night to find himself in unfamiliar places. Unannounced visits by social-service workers had indicated that the home was in physical chaos. There was no organization, the house was untidy and dirty, clothing was strewn on the floor and a menagerie of animals roamed their house. It was evident that meals were unplanned and everyone ate when they were hungry. Dirty dishes were everywhere. Andrew was allowed to eat whenever and whatever he wanted. He never knew what to expect, as there was no predictable schedule. If there were any rules at all, that rule would be "inconsistency." Inconsistency prevailed in that home in almost every area. Love had not been enough.

The myth of Andrew's parents was both absolute and dysfunctional for him. They believed that everyone must be happy. Happiness and goodness were one in their myth. When Andrew came into their life, they had a dream that he would be loving and kind if they could always keep him happy. Everyone in the home, including Andrew, could do what they wanted at any time. As soon as Andrew became a toddler, he was allowed to go to bed when he wanted, destroy whatever he wanted, and behave in any way he desired. He was never taught table manners or normal social behavior. There was no routine. His parents were then free to live their dream of total freedom from the responsibility to keep a clean house or provide Andrew with clean neat clothing. This continued throughout his school years.

The rules of Andrew's myth were: You must not trust anyone. You must put yourself first. You must take what you want, knowing you are the center of the universe. His dream within the myth at home seemed to be that you cannot depend upon anything or anyone. Everyone is free to do whatever they want, whenever they want. It is unnecessary and unsafe to connect with others in a positive way. You cannot depend on anything anyone says. It is not necessary to respect authority. It is okay to lie and cheat. That is the only way to survive. Andrew had taken on the roles of troublemaker, delinquent, and emotionally disturbed person.

This dysfunctional myth caused Andrew to become a juvenile delinquent. It had been taught to him inadvertently by his parents as well as through the video games he played on the internet, which they encouraged him to play whenever he demanded their attention and inconvenienced them in any way.

Andrew's parents were unable to change their own or Andrew's myth as it was so very ingrained in him. They also had been unable to discipline him consistently in any way from the time he was an infant.

Andrew was finally sent to a treatment center for emotionally disturbed teenagers. He was being taught for the first time that he must accept the consequences of his actions. There was no escape. He also learned he was not entitled to everything he wanted. His story continues, but hopefully he will learn to change his myth and find peace and feelings of safety in a new and functional myth.

Functional and dysfunctional myths are at opposite ends of a continuum. Every myth is as different from every other myth as every human being is different from every other human being. Myths can expand without being shattered as individuals within their myth can learn new things if their myth is permeable.

Progressive Myths as a Therapeutic Key

I discovered that viewing human behavior through the lens of Progressive Myths not only enables patients to better understand themselves, but also to understand others and learn to empathize with them. Awareness of their own myths and those of others can reduce self blame and the blaming of others for many of their problems. The progressive myth model is just one key of many that can help human beings recover from traumatic events.

Many patients arrive at my office in a state of extreme emotional suffering. They ask for my help and I want to help them. I think of the progressive myth model as a metaphoric key I can use to unlock the lock to their inner thoughts and views of the world. I am honored to be standing beside them, shedding the light of loving compassion upon them and all the facets of their present myth, as I support them to create a more functional myth and provide tools that enable them to learn new ways to connect with others and interact with the world. That is what therapy is all about.

This model is an extremely helpful therapeutic tool. I have started to use it routinely in my practice, when I feel it is appropriate. I discuss the myths model with a patient, help them identify their own myths and the decisions they made as a result of their personal myth. I then help them determine how whatever problem they are having may be related to it. I will continue to pursue further research related to progressive myths.

The conscious awareness that everyone lives within their own myth, may also help to understand conflicting views within our world. Hopefully, the model of progressive myths could explain the current volatile political viewpoints and negative emotional energies generated from different political viewpoints prevalent today.

My Second Myth

As I began to prepare for college I created my second myth. My second myth was functional, probably absolute, and impermeable.

I first decided that I really would become a doctor like my father, and all would be well. At that time, my mother began to warn me that I must protect my virginity at all costs, in order to secure a good husband at some future time. She said, "If you aren't a virgin when you marry, your husband will never trust you and your marriage will fail." She also stated, "If you have sex before marriage, I will kill myself!" I remember now that I believed her then, but put her pronouncements immediately out of my mind, not to remember them until many years later. (This was long ago, before the sexual revolution, but is a good example of the effects of parental pronouncements upon a teenager who is building her dream.)

The rules in my new myth were: You must study hard in college. You must remain a virgin. You must marry in order to be happy. You must have children, and you must place yourself as less than your husband. His needs come first. Men need to feel superior, so never let anyone know how smart you are, even yourself. After you are married, you must keep a beautiful home and have perfect children. You must protect yourself from men in the meantime. The roles I took on for my new myth were wife, mother, student, housewife.

Basically, I decided that I would get a good education and have the ability to support myself. I also remained very chaste and managed subconsciously to put on extra weight, to protect myself from any possible sexual digressions. I could not get into medical school as at that time, they would not accept women who planned to marry and have children. This mythic dream was explained in my first book, *Mother Bashing: Does She Deserve It?* It was my fairy tale and dream of living happily ever after.

In my senior year of college, I married a law student, shortly before earning a Bachelor's Degree in Nursing. I felt secure and complacent, because I had done everything my myth required, except go to medical school. I accepted the loss of that dream at the time as I desired a "Prince Charming" more than becoming a doctor like my father.

My second myth was destroyed suddenly, when my marriage began to fail. As problems escalated in my relationship with my husband, I decided to return to college. My second myth shattered at that time. In retrospect, I believe I thought I might be able to build a new myth within the marriage. I would get a graduate degree and be free to explore the world. This was something I had always wanted to do, but believed I shouldn't accomplish, while being married.

Graduate school was thrilling, allowing me to be me. I had never felt like I really belonged with any group of people before going to graduate school. Now, I felt unstoppable. The pain and suffering from the deterioration of my marriage was channeled into learning. After earning a Master's Degree in Psychology, I was offered a fellowship to get a Ph.D. I accepted, not realizing all the while, that I would need an entirely new myth.

I earned a Ph.D. three years after the Master's Degree. My husband and I divorced amicably, several years after that. I had become a different person. The benefit of the crisis from breaking that second myth was, for the first time, to give myself the freedom to be my authentic self.

A large number of people are actually able to live their entire lives within their original myths, and experience themselves as "living happily ever after," expanding their myth to adjust to world changes. Still others, like myself, live through many progressive myths.

Crisis is the great myth-buster. Everyone experiences various traumas as they grow to maturity. Belief that things will always be congruent with their myth shatters their myth. When one's myth is shattered, a person must suddenly adjust to a new and different perception of reality. Some mythical beliefs are obviously irrational. Failure to recognize irrational beliefs and release one's attachment to them, leads to continued suffering. Inability to let go of the irrational portion of one's myth prevents individuals from learning from their past mistakes. They must change their perceptions, in order to gain the knowledge and ability to reconfigure their lives around past disappointments, losses, and failures. Individuals will then be free to progress to another, more functional myth or perhaps even go beyond the need to have a myth, if that is possible.

When children and adults become deeply entrenched in various types of irrational myths, it can block the development of resilience and impede the growth of consciousness. High intensity crises have the potential to shatter myths and raise consciousness.

My Third Myth

My third myth was functional and expansive. It was a dream where I visualized myself as single and free to travel the world as well as seek all the intellectual pursuits that I had dreamed about for years. I was happy and felt secure within myself. All was well. My children were almost all out of the "nest." My rules for myself were that I must actualize myself, remain single, and help others. My roles were Scholar, Therapist,

Adventurer, Student. Then a challenge to my myth began to develop.

I was returning from Venezuela where I had presented a week long workshop, and decided to stop in Florida on the way home. I had been invited to join some friends who were staying in a hotel in Miami. I hoped to just rest there for a few days after my workshop before returning home to Ohio. I felt safe and among friends. The morning after I arrived, I met a man in the coffee shop who lived in Milwaukee, Wisconsin. You guessed it! The challenge that caused my myth to expand was falling in love. It took me three years to modify my permeable myth and remarry. I added "Wife" to my previous roles.

The benefit of expanding that myth was in learning that I was lovable, just as I am, even though driven to explore new horizons. I previously thought no man could ever fully accept someone like me as a partner, if he knew who I really was.

After I expanded this myth, I dreamed that my new life would continue forever. I would be free to explore the world, would maintain my health, and I would have companionship for the rest of my life. That myth was shattered when my husband Jack died of a sudden heart attack right before my eyes. I caught him as he fell to the floor and gave him CPR until the emergency squad arrived. It was futile.

I was thrust into a high intensity crisis, never before having experienced gut-wrenching grief like that in the past. It was about six years before I began to create another myth. During that time I continued to explore the nature of reality and search for greater understanding of who I really was. Once again, I was between myths.

The things I learned from the shattering of my third myth were that life and relationships are finite; it is imperative to be in the here and now as much as possible; and that all relationships end, so we must cherish them while we have them.

When exploring the question, "What is reality?" I came upon the work of John Hagelin, a quantum physicist who has studied quantum field theory. He demonstrated through the use of string theory, the existence of a universal base of "all that is." He described it as teeming with manifest energy and all intelligence. Could this be reality? It seemed to describe the heightened sense of consciousness I experienced in the hospital.

His findings are congruent with my experiences right before my surgery. Many people have reported experiences such as these when faced with death or after near death experiences. Could this universal base of "all that is" be the location of the universal energy of love and peace?

People who can either expand their myths to incorporate the knowledge of others in their myths and beyond, or experience progressive myths as I did, have the opportunity to access and share this light with others in all the groups we touch with our myths.

My Fourth Myth

My fourth progressive myth began to be formed when I decided to leave Wisconsin and find a place where I could live among kindred souls. After looking all around the country, I chose Santa Fe, New Mexico. I decided that I would be free to explore all my interests here. I would meditate regularly and use all the alternative health care methods I knew to maintain good health. I planned to live to be at least one hundred years old. (Most of my mother's family had lived into their nineties.) My rules and roles were basically the same as my third myth, with the added learnings from the loss of it.

I was open to a new relationship, but knew I really didn't need one. Life would be good for the rest of my life. I would need no one.

As you now know, that myth was shattered by my journey to the door of death. I learned so much from it.

I learned how to receive love, even when I couldn't give love and felt unlovable and helpless. I learned I was not invincible and neither I, nor anyone else, can really control anything, no matter how hard we try. I became aware of how fragile my life and all life really is. I believe my consciousness was raised to a higher level than ever before. Most of the time, I can experience greater connectedness and oneness with everything and everyone, as well as understand and accept all people, whoever and wherever they are, with no judgement. I learned that love is the only reality for me.

The model of progressive myths illustrates how we are all embedded within many myths. Each human being has their own myth as well as shares part of themselves within many other myths.

If you visualize concentric circles with you in the middle, you realize that around you, are the myths of your family, and beyond that, your work group, your neighborhood, your city, your state, your country, your hemisphere, the whole world, all of humankind, the planet.

Yes, you share myths with all of humanity. Imagine, if all myths were expandable and permeable, everyone could learn from one another, understand one another, and experience loving compassion for one another. Consider the possible impact of one enlightened person in the middle of their concentric circle!

I learned many things from the destruction of my myths. Their shattering enabled me to find out who I really am and gave me courage to explore the world. I discovered that I am lovable for who I am, and learned to accept the finiteness of everything in life. The here-and-now is all we really have and I now know without doubt that I am in control of nothing. The shattering caused suffering, which gave me the opportunity to grow.

My Present Myth

I am lying on my bed, resting. It is late afternoon and the sun's rays are long gone from the windows on this side of the house. It is quiet here now and I'm taking a break from my work. (I've almost completed this book about my journey to the door of death.) I'm feeling well physically and emotionally and pondering what dream my present myth is about.

I'll share my new myth with you. It is related to the revelations I had right before my surgery. My dream is that love is all there is. We are all interconnected. Everyone can be conscious of, and understand, everyone else. We are also one with all life on this planet. There must be world peace. The rules of my myth are simple. Tap into that reservoir of love. It is also within you. Learn to forgive and empathize with all others within their myths at all levels. You will then have everything you really need and want. I feel blessed to have learned these things that I only imagined before. Now they are deeply embedded in my heart. I am truly a better human being as a result of my journey to the door of death.

References

Newberg, Andrew and Waldman, Mark. 2009. *How God Changes your Brain.* New York: Ballantine Books.

Viereack, George S. "What Life Means to Einstein." *The Saturday Evening Post.* October 26, 1929. P17.

Schilpp, Paul Arthur, editor. 1970. *Albert Einstein: Philosopher-Scientist.* Open Court Publishing: LaSalle. Third edition.

Frankl, Victor.1959. *Man's Search for Meaning.* Boston: Beacon Press. Boston.

Zinn, John Kabbat. 2012. *Mindfulness for Beginners.* Boston: Sounds True. Boston.

Chopra, Depak. 2013, *God: A Story of Revelation.* New York: Harper Collins.

Wolf, Fred Alan.1994 *The Dreaming Universe.* New York: Wolf Productions.

Hagelin, J.S. 1987. "Is Consciousness the Unified Field? A Field Theorist's Perspective." *Modern Science and Vedic Science.* pp. 29-87.

Watts, Alan. 1961. *Psychotherapy East and West.* New York: Random House.

Maslow, Abraham. 1964. *Religion, Values, and Peak Experiences.* Ohio State University: Cleveland.

Maslow, Abraham. 1971. *The Farther Reaches of Human Nature.* New York: Viking Press

Campbell, Joseph. 1988. *The Power of Myth.* New York: Viking.

Campbell, Joseph. 2004. *Pathways To Bliss: Mythology and Personal Transformation.* Novato, California: Joseph Campbell foundation.

Campbell, Joseph. 2008. *The Hero With a Thousand Faces.* Novato, California: Joseph Campbell Foundation.

Alter, R.M. and Alter, J. 2000. *The Transformative Power of Crisis: Our Journey to Psychological Healing and spiritual Awakening.* New York: Regan Books.

Jung, C.G., Adler, and Hull, R.F.D. "The Archetypes and the Collective Unconscious." Vol. 9, part 1. *The Collected Works of CG Jung.* New York: Princeton University Press.

Jung, C.G. 1958. *The Undiscovered Self.* New York: Little, Brown, and Company, Inc.

Ross, Elizabeth-Kubler MD and Kessler, David. 2005 *On Grief and Grieving, Finding the Twelve stages of Loss.* New York: Scribner.

Lukerman, Alex, MD. 2012. *The Undefeated Mind: On the Science of Constructing an Indestructible Self.* Delafield Beach, Florida: Health Communications, inc.

Braude, Stephen. 2005. *Imortal Remains: The Evidence for Life After Death.* Latham, Maryland: Roman and Littlefield.

Seibert, Al. Ph.D. 2005 *the Resiliency Advantage.* San Francisco: Barret-Koehler Publishers.

Feldman, David B. Ph.D. and Kravetz, Lee David. 2014. *Super survivors: The surprising Link Between Suffering and Success.* New York: Harper Collins.

Hawkins, David R.M.D., Ph.D. 2007. *Discovery of the Presence of God.* Sedona, Arizona: Veritas Publishing.

Radin, Dean, Ph.D. 20013. *Supernormal: Science, Yoga, and The evidence for Extraordinary Psychic Abilities.* New York: Random House.

Radin, Dean. 2006. *Entangled Minds.* New York: Simon and Schuster

Ruiz, Don Miguel. 2012. *The Four Agreements.* San Rafael, California: Amber-Allen Publishing.

Davidson R. J. and Harrington, A. (Eds). 2001. *Visions of Compassion: Western Scientists and Tibetan Buddhists Examine Human Nature.* New York: Oxford Press.

Houshmand, Z., Livingston, R.B. and Wallace, A.B. (Eds). 2007. *Conciousness at the Crossroads: Conversations with the Dalai Lama on Brain Science and Buddhism* Ithaca, New York: Snow Lion Publications.

Ratree Sudsuang, Vilai Chantaney, Kongdej Veluvan. 1991. "Effect of Buddhist Meditation on serum cortisol and total protein levels, blood pressure, pulse rate, lung volume. and reaction time." *Physiology and Behavior. Volulme 50, Issue 3, P543-548.*

Russel, Peter. 2002. *From Science to God: A Physicist's Journey into the Mystery of Consciousness.* Novato, California: New World Library.

Tolle, Eckhardt. 1999. *The Power of Now.* Vancover, B.C.: Namaste Publishing

About the Author

Dr. Nancy E. Perry is a Clinical Psychologist as well as a Registered Nurse, author, and artist. She earned her B.S. degree in Nursing, M.A. and Ph.D. degrees in Psychology at the Ohio State University. Her Associate's Degree in Fine Arts was earned at the Santa Fe Community College in New Mexico. Dr. Perry has served on the faculty of the Ohio State University, The University of Wisconsin, and the Wisconsin Professional School of Psychology.

She is well recognized throughout the world for her work with Trauma Victims and Dissociative Disorders and has presented papers and workshops in many countries on these topics. Her last book was, *Mother Bashing: Does She Deserve It?* Dr. Perry currently resides in Santa Fe, New Mexico.

Proof

Made in the USA
Charleston, SC
21 January 2017